# *A Tale of Two Cabins*

## *Comparative Stories of Thoreau's Cabin, Nature and Life*

# *A Tale of Two Cabins*

## *Comparative Stories of Thoreau's Cabin, Nature and Life*

*John Irving Clapp*

5/19/21

to: Joe & Lauria

Thanks for staying with us.

*Levellers Press*

AMHERST, MASSACHUSETTS

Published by *Levellers Press*, Amherst, Massachusetts

Printed in the United States of America

ISBN 978-1-937146-80-1

*This book is dedicated to my brother-in-law,*
*Garry Anderson,*
*who taught me much about the woods*
*and the animals who reside within them.*
*1939 – 2015*

*Gone too,*
*My old friend, Allen "Zippy" Bardwell*
*1942 – 2015*

*Man's Best Friend*
*Baxter, devoted pet, faithful hiking partner*
*October 18, 2015*

# *Contents*


| | | |
|---|---|---|
| Preface | | ix |
| Acknowledgments | | xi |
| Introduction xiii | | |
| Chapter 1 | A Spot for the Cabin | 1 |
| Chapter 2 | The Trickster | 3 |
| Chapter 3 | Walden Inspiration | 6 |
| Chapter 4 | Let the Construction Begin | 15 |
| Chapter 5 | Finishing the Cabin: The Story of a Door | 21 |
| Chapter 6 | Ides of March, 2014 | 32 |
| Chapter 7 | Mt. Tom and the New Village of Northampton | 34 |
| Chapter 8 | A la mode for the Abode | 37 |
| Chapter 9 | A Shack up in the Woods: A Tribute to Jack | 39 |
| Chapter 10 | House on the Hill | 49 |
| Chapter 11 | Early Concerns, Present Danger | 53 |
| Chapter 12 | Conservation | 57 |
| Chapter 13 | Encounters in the Wild | 61 |
| Chapter 14 | Slither, Creep and Crawl | 67 |
| Chapter 15 | Plants, Moss and Ferns | 73 |
| Chapter 16 | Sauntering | 75 |
| Chapter 17 | Northampton and Concord Connections Abolition and Utopian Communities | 78 |
| Chapter 18 | Transcendentalism and Religion | 82 |
| Chapter 19 | 'Ne'er-do-well or Mystic? | 88 |
| Chapter 20 | Puritan Work Ethic? | 90 |
| Chapter 21 | Death of a Poet | 98 |
| Chapter 22 | A Thoreauvian Father's Day | 102 |
| About the Author | | 107 |
| Bibliography | | 108 |

# *Preface*

My goal in writing this book is to describe the process of building my cabin and how it compares to Thoreau building his Walden cabin. The story is about the similarities of each structure, and the differences in building techniques as they relate to the 170-year time difference. Since I do not keep journals, I had to rely upon my memory of encounters with nature from years past, and more recently from reading works about, and by Thoreau in the transcendentalist movement.

I have tried to compare some of my ideas with Thoreau's thoughts on nature, religion, death, wildlife, Native American life, land preservation and cultural differences. The story is part autobiographical, part historical, with a bit of local natural history thrown in, plus my own reflections on transcendentalist thought.

Like Thoreau, I have always been drawn to nature and have picked areas either in the woods or in a meadow on the edge of the woods, as locations for the two homes I have built for myself over the years. My favorite pastimes always included being in natural settings. For example, my wife, son, and I would head out after work for an overnight of backpacking and camping, or I would go off by myself to spend a winter's night atop a local mountain range. Having the Deerfield River located practically in our backyard made it easy for us to include a white water canoe trip a few times a week. Rock climbing and biking were excellent excuses to get out and enjoy our natural surroundings. All of these excursions satisfied my lifelong attraction to nature.

As I was completing my reproduction of Thoreau's cabin, I invited my friend Donald to visit it. As a fellow Thoreauvian I felt that, of all the people I know, he would appreciate it the most. I have known Don for twenty-five years but not as a professor of English and the former director of the UMass Amherst graduate writing program. Instead, I know him from my contracting business and trading my skills as a carpenter for a week's stay each summer at his vacation home on Swans Island, Maine. I would spend the week with my wife Dee, and our son Jarred, doing small carpentry jobs or repairs while the ocean waves lapped the shore just forty feet away.

After showing Don my cabin he encouraged me to write the story of its process. I took him up on his suggestion. Upon Don's first reading of *A Tale of Two Cabins*, from which I received positive feedback and encouragement to publish, he asked if I had a next book in mind and I explained that if I did it would have to be the tale of the kidnapping of my fifth great-grandmother by the French and Indians during the 1704 raid on Deerfield, Massachusetts, which I talk briefly about later in the current story.

Writing this book has been a great journey for me and I regard it as one of the highlights of my sixty-five years on this planet.

# *Acknowledgments*

I wish to thank Donald Junkins and his wife Kaimei Zheng: Donald for encouraging me to write this book and for his many edits, and Kaimei for the cover design.

I want to extend my appreciation to:

- My sister Lorraine Clapp-O'Keefe, and our friend and historian, Barbara Pelissier for their punctuation and grammar checks,
- Naturalist Molly Hale for reviewing the natural history sections of this book.
- Our friend, poet Jody Cothey for starting me off in the right direction,
- Physicist Colin Fredericks for his input on Quantum Entanglement,
- Brooks Ballenger, fellow "disobedient" for help in recollecting the Seabrook protest,
- Also, special thanks to Mark Majeski for allowing me to use his Seabrook photos, and to Fresh Water Mussel Alan Kelly for putting us together.

And to my son, Jarred, an excellent writer himself, thanks for listening and commenting on each chapter as it was written. To my wife of twenty-five years, the love of my life and Best Mate, thanks for allowing me to read you each day's writing over the phone on your way home from work. Even though I sometimes didn't want to hear her critiques, she was usually right in the end.

# *Introduction*

by Donald Junkins

This is an extraordinary book, Yankee in flavor and tone, and full of the juxtapositions between personal family histories, local historic personalities, and odd jobbing leading up to the building of secluded cabins by both John Clapp and Henry Thoreau. As such, John, in his own biographical quest to live and leave a record of his own life in rural western Massachusetts, is amply Thoreauvian. In his detailed style and in his interests, John Clapp takes as his post-midlife imagistic pursuit the life behind Henry Thoreau's own nineteenth-century erection of his cabin on the shore of Walden Pond in Concord, Massachusetts where he lived for two years, two months, and two days. In *A Tale of Two Cabins*, Clapp details costs and building procedures as they parallel and as they differ from Thoreau's own details in the first chapter, "Economy" in *Walden, or Life in the Woods.* Whereas Thoreau additionally adds an almost veiled tongue-in-cheek explanation on his title page to introduce his book,

> *"I do not propose to write an ode to dejection, but to brag as lustily as chanticleer in the morning, standing on his roost, if only to wake my neighbors up"*

John Clapp simply states that he has tried in his own book to compare some of his ideas to those of Thoreau on the subjects of nature, religion, death, wildlife, Native American life, land preservation and cultural differences. What John adds are the unique details of his personal biography which underlie and inform his decision to emulate the economical and environmental motivations that guided Thoreau in his singular attempt to build and dwell in a cabin in the woods for a substantial period of time. John's intent is rigorously clear in its conception, his writing style is forthright, and he achieves and declares a philosophy of individual initiative and family values. The project writes itself into an illuminative achievement.

Thoreau's anecdotal and Yankee-shrewd *Walden*, divided into eighteen different subjects in chapters ranging from eight to seventy-four pages each (the first and last chapters) covers various subjects such as Solitude, Visitors, Winter Animals, and his own Bean Fields, and reflects on his own self-built Walden cabin. John Clapp's book divides into twenty-two chapters that cover such subjects as Walden Inspiration; Finishing the Cabin...the Story of the Door; Encounters in the Wild; Plants, Moss and Ferns; Transcendentalism and religion; and A Thoreauvian Father's Day.

John Clapp's tale, unlike Thoreau's, stems directly from his own memory (Thoreau's *Walden* leaned heavily on his own journals leading up to his Walden Pond stay) and his own research into his Clapp family history, plus his own earlier life leading up to his active retirement from the carpentry business. Whereas Thoreau's view from his cabin doorstep allowed him the near shore of the pond and one section of the pond itself, John can see through the hardwood forest as far distant as Mt. Tom, ten miles southeast in Easthampton. John's description of this view represents beautifully the tone and the detailed sensitivities that John relied on in the evolution of his book:

"Perhaps John Clapp has even out-Thoreaued Thoreau. In chapter eight, titled "A la Mode for the Abode," John writes of his own cabin in the woods,

> *"To top off the cabin, I installed a single 110 watt solar panel which I had salvaged from my sister's house. I built a one foot by two foot pine box in which I placed two six-volt deep cycle batteries for storage and a charge controller that allows the batteries to be fully charged without over-charging. The system produces enough electricity for a single 20 watt DC light bulb and a DC outlet for charging a laptop. "Methinks" this would have met with the approval of Thoreau."*

In the final chapter of *A Tale of Two Cabins*, John Clapp narrates a recent Father's Day trip to Concord during which John and his son Jarred not only paddled a section of the Concord River in honor of Thoreau's book, *A Week on the Concord and Merrimack Rivers*, but visited the original site of Thoreau's cabin on the shore of Walden Pond and placed a stone on the cairn of stones beside the site, an idea begun by Bronson Alcott, father of Louisa May Alcott and close friend of Thoreau himself. Inscribed on the stone was simply "John and Jarred, 2014, Father's Day."

As Thoreau said in *Walden*, "Simplicity, simplicity, simplicity."

*Chapter One*

# *A Spot for the Cabin*

*There are none happy in the world but beings who enjoy freely a vast horizon.*

Demodara (Krishna)

I am finally out in the woods to just sit, enjoy and observe. All my previous visits to date, besides the building process, involved a quick stop-off on a hike, a brief stay with guests or family, or to fire up the potbelly stove to cure the freshly-applied stove black. It's been two years since I brought the first stick of lumber up here. Every piece of wood, large and small, joists, rafters and studs, windows, siding, roofing and flooring all were hauled here on my Kubota tractor a quarter of a mile from the house over a woodland trail.

After picking a spot for the cabin I cleared a small area, careful not to remove any trees that might block the north wind or help shade me from the summer sun. I intentionally left a few oak and hickory trees on either side to frame the cabin visually. I wanted it to appear as organic as possible; nestled on a side hill. The cabin indeed now looks like it just grew from the spores of a mushroom.

I chose my view from the front window to face southeast to take advantage of the skyline of Mt. Tom in Easthampton, ten miles away as the crow flies. This was a sight we were unaware of until, on a hike one sunny fall day after the leaves had dropped, we spied the now familiar outline of the ridge through the trees. We were thrilled with our discovery. Downslope I removed fifteen trees which revealed a most spectacular expanse of rolling hills and the mountain beyond. No other spot on our 120 acres could have afforded us this perspective. Not a single sign of civilization is visible between here and Mt. Tom except on the top of the ridge where there are a few radio towers and a single windmill that no longer spins. Early settlers must have seen this exact expansive vista of pristine woodlands, minus the modern metal.

Mt. Tom has a distinctive ridge line that drops off rather abruptly on the south end. It was formed near the end of the Triassic Period from a lava intrusion which solidified into a basalt ridge some 300 feet thick, now rising to 1200 feet due to millions of years of tilting and erosion. The cliff side that faces my cabin is nearly devoid of foliage and is sheer rock. The rust color takes its hue from the iron content in the basalt. When exposed to the elements it oxidizes much like a nail or bolt rusts after it's been left outside in the rain. The cliffs are home to both Copperhead snakes and Timber Rattlers. They are rare and seldom seen, although a man was bitten by a Copperhead a few years ago. To me, these poisonous snakes create the potential for danger and make the mountain all the more alluring.

*Chapter Two*

# *The Trickster*

As I write, in the periphery of my vision, a dark figure catches my attention; a large canine in pursuit of a meal passes not forty feet from my window. It is an Eastern coyote, a hybrid of the smaller Western coyote that interbred with wolves from the Northern Great Lakes region as they migrated north and east. The coyotes in New England now look more like wolves than their Western counterpart. They have gradually made New England their home, taking the place of the wolves of the 1800s which were eradicated by the early settlers because they helped themselves to the farmer's sheep and calves. I would have sided with the wolves because I don't eat mutton or veal, and wool makes me itch. We hear the coyotes in the night, a combination of howling, barking, and yipping that makes the hair on the back of my neck tingle with instinctual fear. I usually open the windows for full effect.

We have lost three family cats over a ten-year span to these beautiful beasts and mourned each one, but this area is the coyotes' haunt now and we share it with them. In a way I am honored to help fill their bellies, but we have stopped acquiring cats.

I have always offered up the carcasses of our goats, loved pets that had lived out their lives and peacefully slipped away in the night, dragging their bodies on a sled through the deep snow to an appropriate spot at the edge of the forest, a similar chore given to me by my father in years past.

Growing up on a dairy farm, it was my job to take the lifeless bodies of stillborn calves to the woods for a carnivorous burial. Those calves were brought to a wooded area one hundred yards behind the barn, pulled by bailer twine looped around their hind legs, their small, thin corpses undulating as they passed over uneven ground, the grass still wet from the morning dew. As a kid I was probably a bit taken aback by the whole ordeal, but in retrospect I recognize it as the ultimate in recycling, and I would not want to deprive these wild animals of a much needed meal.

Back in the late 1950s there were no coyotes. They arrived in the late 1960s and they were quite numerous by the '70s and '80s. We used to refer to them as coy dogs but more than likely they were wolf/coyote hybrids. Instead, it was foxes along with bobcats, crows and fisher cats that would dine on my offerings. I remember hearing the fox, a yip of a bark, a communication, perhaps to a potential mate or the mom calling her kits back to the den. My thoughts were often, "what a wild, cool place, a den of foxes not a quarter of a mile from our house."

If it wasn't illegal, at my own passing, I would feel it appropriate to offer up my remains for the taking, deep in the woods that I love. This was a common and acceptable practice among some Native American tribes, particularly the Plains Indians and tribes of the Pacific Northwest. Perhaps more interesting is the celestial burial still practiced by Tibetan Buddhists where the "undertaker" transports the loved one's body to a mountain outcrop or a pastoral meadow and starts a hemlock bough fire. To the local vultures the smell of burning hemlock would indicate that a meal is being prepared. The administrator of the rite removes the flesh of the departed, going so far as to break up the bones into small pieces and mixing them with millet, enabling the birds to carry off all of the remains. The Buddhist belief is that only after all the remains are carried off to the sky can the soul be released for its final passage.

This rite, called *Jhator,* is performed at dawn out of sight of the deceased's family, although the rest of the community is encouraged to witness the act to remind them of, and reinforce their belief in, reincarnation; that the body is a temporary vessel which the soul inhabits until death occurs. This practice is still the preferred burial method of the less wealthy Buddhists. If they can afford to they have their loved ones cremated, and the wealthiest might be interred in a *stupa.*

The *Jhator* seems a bit shocking to our western sensibility, but is an acceptable practice to believers in such rituals. I would not put any family members that survive me through such procedures, but I believe it would be an appropriate choice. I would choose the option of cremation with my ashes spread to the wind at my favorite spots in nature.

*Chapter Three*

# *Walden Inspiration*

---

### *"Old Cedar"*

*Through the window it takes up two panes, a short distance at the edge of the forest.*
*Silver/gray totem stands ghost-like in defiance.*
*Death overcame, perhaps in my youth.*
*Still standing, firmly rooted, its bark has long been shed.*
*No cambium layer to nourish it.*
*It's on its own.*
*Relies on its resinous nature.*
*Trunk, branches gnarled and weathered, it resists decay.*
*Its conifer cousin long ago fell, rotted and fed the forest floor.*
*While standing, they were abode to grubs and ants, a smorgasbord for the Pileated Woodpecker, its rap, rap, rapping resonating through the woods.*
*Still a house on the ground rotting, musty, pungent forest smell, a myriad of insects, larva, microorganisms feast until it becomes earth.*
*Not the cedar.*
*Lived fifty years-stands in death fifty more.*
*Defiant.*
*Cut into its heartwood, rose/pink, fragrant, vibrant as if still alive, retains the better part of youth.*
*Cut it down, use it for fence posts it will last fifty years or more.*
*Barbed wire will rust, as a post it remains strong.*
*Aromatic, in a closet, repels moths for generations.*
*I will let them stand to be admired by my son for years to come.*
*I will let them stand; cedar does not grow wild here anymore.*

—John Clapp

---

Mt. Tom, snow covered, takes on a pinkish hue as the sun sets, combining with the snow-covered forest floor, and in stark contrast to the dark green hemlock and pine understory, one can only sink deeply into the tranquility of the moment. If I could only eliminate the blinking lights atop the radio towers which become more intrusive as darkness overcomes the scene. All things considered, a small price to pay for such an expanse of beauty.

I first became acquainted with Thoreau's work in the late 1970s although it was only in the past few years that I immersed myself in his writing. After many visits to Walden and to Concord, I decided to build a replica of Thoreau's cabin in the woods next to my house. I had no Walden Pond, but a clear view of the valley and mountain range beyond.

In the sixties Thoreau's books inspired many of that generation to experience a simpler way of life. *Walden* became a handbook; actually a primer for the back-to-nature movement with its anti-establishment reverberations. His books raised the consciousness of many. Activists took his words and wisdom as a call-to-arms to practice civil disobedience, a way to protest what they considered to be unfair and unjust practices. The protests ran the gamut from anti-war and pro-civil rights marches to conservation of land and later the anti-nuke movement, of which I was a part. They read the teachings of the Hindu and Buddhist masters that brought into focus things that they thought should be assimilated into our western ways; to live without the extravagances that the post-war economy afforded us. "Simplify, Simplify" was their mantra and Thoreau was their mentor. Martin Luther King Jr. and Mahatma Gandhi were influenced by Thoreau's essay *Civil Disobedience*.

My personal experience with non-violent protest occurred in 1979 during the movement to expand nuclear power. The nuke plant at Seabrook, New Hampshire was well into construction when I read a flyer inviting individuals to attend a meeting to plan an action of civil disobedience at the new plant. The action focused on an attempt to overwhelm the fences and occupy the construction site in the hope of disrupting and halting the progress.

The "meeting" coalesced into a tight-knit group after weeks of non-violent training which included how to properly respond to police aggression in ways that would not escalate potential violence, essentially sitting down and linking arms. Through these meetings I learned the "fine art" of reaching consensus in decision making. I concur with fellow protester, Brooks, that "striving for perfect consensus leads to paralysis. People would have all day meetings just to decide what to do that day. For a group to function there needs to be democratic leadership." This juxtaposed to the proper way to put on and adjust our own gas masks, which we purchased from an army and navy surplus store. In addition to the mask, we were to carry a squirt bottle of saline solution to use if someone was sprayed in the eyes with pepper spray or came into contact with tear gas, the favorite weapons used by police to disperse a crowd of protesters. They were also known for the liberal use of night sticks.

The action was orchestrated by the Direct Action Coalition, an offshoot of the New England-based Clamshell Alliance. The leadership of the Clamshell Alliance opposed this action because they believed it was too militant. Unfortunately the Seabrook action was lacking in leadership, partly as a result of the consensus model. Because our group volunteered to do communications, we were assumed to be organizers which we definitely were not, but we were able to muddle through.

We called our affinity group the Fresh Water Mussels, as we were the inland version of the salt water clams from which Clamshell Alliance got its name. Our logo was a muscular arm, flexed at the elbow, with the hand made into a fist projecting from a mussel shell. Someone made up head bands with our logo on the front which we were to wear during the protest so we could quickly identify each other. I don't remember if anyone wore them but it made a nice souvenir. The protest had been planned for October 6, 1979 and we arrived in Seabrook the night before, setting up camp on a piece of property adjacent to the power plant.

Hundreds of protesters arrived to participate that day to show their opposition to this hazardous form of power, and we were all prepared to be arrested. The first day, many of us lined up along the chain-link fence which ran the perimeter of the plant, with bolt cutters at the ready. As we waited for instructions from the organizers, the police took advantage of the moment and a dozen cops appeared behind us and proceeded to confiscate our bolt cutters by tossing them to the opposite side of the fence. Our plan was to use these cutters to open holes in the fence to gain access to the plant. Luckily, there were many more. Unfortunately, I had come down with a stomach bug which weakened me significantly to the point that I lost my balance and fell into the arms of a cop. He helped me upright and commented, "be careful or you will die before the nuclear radiation can get you." I recovered quickly enough and was able to join the plan of action we were given.

Our group split up the first morning, half going to the railroad tracks to create a diversion while the others participated in an action to block the main gate of the plant. They had been warned that the State Police would use water cannons to disperse the protesters. Some folks left but others decided to stand their ground, while supporters took up a collection of raincoats to help them stay dry. When the police rolled out their water cannons the protesters hunkered down in a kneeling fetal position to make a smaller target and withstand the extreme force. Fortunately for the group, water pressure was weak at Seabrook and their water cannons could produce a stream of water not much stronger than a garden hose. After a few minutes people stood up, laughing and dancing at their meager attempt at dispersing the crowd. Charlie, one of the Mussels, offered his backside as target practice.

That night the group decided to sleep in front of the gate to maintain the blockade. This was a cold wet sleep but they all survived. At one point a van pulled up and a wild-eyed young man rushed out and tried to convince the protesters to climb the fence and tear down an American flag that was prominently displayed inside the gate. When he saw that he was getting nowhere with this idea, he rushed back into the van and drove off. They all assumed that this was an "agent provocateur," a police or FBI plant hoping to discredit our action.

Our task that day involved creating a diversion on the north side while a significant attempt was being made from the south to cut fences and occupy the site. We were to follow a railroad track that led into the plant in a diversionary tactic which involved approaching the gate at the end of the tracks. We pulled a number of small logs from the surrounding forest to make the authorities believe we were a serious threat. The hope was that we would draw the police away from the south side which would help the other group to gain access. The railroad track was above a large marshy area that extended east and west on both sides of the tracks, making it open and vulnerable. The State Police sent out a helicopter to try and disperse the protesters, although it seemed to be an attempt at isolating one of the organizers who they probably identified with binoculars from inside the fence. The man somehow ended up in the marsh making it easy for the helicopter to continually dive at him, eventually driving him back to the woods.

We learned that our attempted diversion failed when one of our runners brought us the news. The use of runners was a way of communicating with one another that avoided the chance of a Walkie-talkie conversation being intercepted. No cell phones back then. We made a valiant attempt and regrouped at the campsite to discuss the plans for the following day.

We were all eager to start the new day's attempt to occupy, and after a breakfast of G.O.R.P. (good old raisins and peanuts) and hard-boiled eggs, we all made our way to the south fence where we were joined by other groups. We had learned of another failed attempt by an affinity group whose goal was to cut through the fence near the main gate. Their job was to be the first wave and absorb the challenge by the police wielding night sticks and spraying tear gas. They were well-equipped with football helmets, gas masks, shoulder pads, cups, knee and shin guards and lots of adrenalin, but apparently were no match for the swarms of local and state police and the National Guard. Although this seemed to be dancing on the edge of non-violence, and indeed critics viewed this as too provocative, they were committed to keeping it peaceful while pressing the issue.

That morning we were organized to make an attempt at the south fence. This was our first try at cutting through the fence, and our affinity group was experiencing some apprehension but we had been well trained and knew how to respond to the wrath of the police. We were all dedicated to the anti-nuke movement and wanted to do what we could to advance our agenda, even if it turned out to be only symbolic. By late morning, we started to move to our designated areas to open multiple holes in the fence, which would hopefully allow hundreds of protesters to stream through, overwhelming the police. Once in, we were to find a suitable area where we could regroup, sit down and settle in for the long haul and began the occupation. We had food and water enough for a few days; after that it would be anybody's guess, we would leave it up to the organizers to resupply us. When we were in position, we all donned our gas masks and our team began work to open a hole in the fence. The police used pepper spray thorough the chain link fence, but wearing long sleeves and gas masks it had little effect on us which infuriated them. My job was to join others to rip down the chain link after the cutters finished their task, while avoiding having our fingers smashed by police wielding their clubs from the other side. With the fence all but cut through we were poised to break in when the tables turned. The cops in riot gear pushed their way out through the opening that we made in an aggressive stampede of uniforms overwhelming us in a crushing show of force.

In our hasty retreat, with the police at our back, frustrated that their pepper spray was ineffective, they started ripping gas masks off the heads of any protester they could catch, throwing the masks to the ground and smashing the lenses with their night sticks. They did not spare the night sticks on us. In the chaos, a fellow "Mussel" did not get his mask on in time and received a dose of pepper spray directly in his eyes, momentarily blinding him. In my panic, with my flight response in full gear, I hesitated and thought, do I help Allen or save myself? Out of the corner of my eye I saw Allen being pummeled with a night stick while he blindly struggled to get away by climbing up an embankment. Altruism won out and I grabbed him by the shirt, pulling him to the safety of a more level surface. After rinsing his eyes with saline solution we ran clear of the cops and their night sticks. I somehow avoided the clubbing and still had a gas mask with the lenses intact. This was far beyond the realm of anything I thought I would ever be involved in and I was relieved that no one was seriously hurt. I think most of us were not terribly disappointed that we didn't get a chance to shut down the plant, but instead felt

that we had succeeded in drawing attention to our mission by helping raise awareness of what we perceived to be an extremely dangerous source of energy.

In retrospect, I cannot be angry with the cops. They were hired by the Seabrook Nuclear Power Plant and the state to protect their property. Although I disagree with their methods, they were doing their job and we were destroying property and attempting to trespass. This was the degree of protest we chose and we knew what the consequences could be. Instead, I blame the nuclear industry for pushing an unsafe source of power on "we the people." History has proved that it was not "too cheap to meter" but was also a deadly decision that cost many lives and destroyed countless more, with vast areas of land made uninhabitable for hundreds of years, and hundreds of square miles of ocean so contaminated with radiation that any fish that survived cannot be consumed. Even though these horrific tragedies in Fukushima and Chernobyl have faded from the headlines, the untold destruction continues to affect thousands of people. We should all learn from these experiences and not trust the oil and gas companies who tell us that the XL pipeline and fracking will be safe. In the next twenty or thirty years, we do not want to witness a major leak over the Ogallala aquifer, making the water undrinkable for millions of people. These accidental leaks happen quite frequently and do irreparable damage to the environment. There have already been a number of earthquakes which scientists have attributed to fracking. These companies will become filthy rich and the people will inherit a filthy planet.

Ironically, no state in the country, no matter how remote, is now willing to become a repository for the highly radioactive spent fuel rods. This waste stays radioactive for 240,000 years and some estimate a million years! As a result, power plants have no place to send it, including plants that have already been decommissioned. Western Massachusetts has two used-up plants within a fifty mile radius. Decades of waste will have to be kept cool, on site, for years and then put in dry cast storage indefinitely, making them a target for terrorists and increase the long-term chance of radiation leaking into the environment.

Our affinity group continued to meet regularly, and we planned another action for the following spring. This time the focus was on Wall Street, our goal being to shut it down. It was largely symbolic, attempting to draw attention to the companies who were investing in the nuclear industry, perhaps embarrassing them into divesting. My friend Jack allowed us a spot on the floor of his Brooklyn loft the night before, so we all got a good night's sleep. To blend in, we all wore suits and ties the day of the action. As we made our way to lower Manhattan that morning, I purchased a copy of *The Wall Street Journal* and tucked it under my arm to give my disguise some added credibility. I actually don't think anyone was fooled as there were many hippy types which suits could not hide. We got to the stock exchange and surrounded the building, linking arms and denying access. My recollection is that the whole event stayed non-violent, although police on horseback tried to intimidate us by attempting to drive their mounts through our line which we were able to hold strong. I believe that the horses had more sense than the cops as they were quite gentle about where they placed their hooves even though they were pushed hard by their riders, apparently not wanting to step on anyone. While we thwarted many that day, most of the essential workers and traders, who had been tipped off, had shown up early, long before the first protesters arrived and were safely inside.

Again, our victory was symbolic in bringing awareness to the issue with plenty of media coverage. This had been the year that I was politicized to acts of civil disobedience as a form of protest. It wasn't until years later that I realized that it was Thoreau who had coined the phrase after spending a night in jail for refusing to pay a poll tax that supported the Mexican War which he adamantly opposed.

*Chapter Four*

# *Let the Construction Begin*

Reading *Walden* gives one a pretty good idea of what his cabin looked like, its dimensions, window and door placement etc., although it was very helpful to me to have found a set of framing plans at the gift store at Walden Pond. These plans had been drawn up by Roland Robbins, an archaeologist who discovered the original site of Thoreau's cabin in 1945, exactly one hundred years to the day after Thoreau moved in. Checking out the reproduction at Walden Pond also helped tremendously. I wanted my cabin to be a close representation, although I did forgo the intricate mortise and tenon joints in the structural beams, and I skipped the dove-tailed joists which got covered by the interior walls and flooring, as it doesn't detract from the structural integrity of the framing. From the finished interior one cannot see that I took a quicker route.

I had been collecting material for years, saving odds and ends that I might use one day. This included twelve-over-twelve, double-hung windows salvaged from my parents' house which was originally built in 1894. The windows were kept in storage for eighteen years. I was not sure if I would ever use them, I only knew that I didn't want to throw them away. Coincidently, these were exactly the style of windows in Thoreau's cabin.

Before I could start framing the cabin I needed to determine the size of the window openings, as framing the walls depended upon this. On a hot summer day before starting construction, I brought the windows into the cool of the cellar to be refurbished, replacing the damaged sills and giving them a fresh coat of paint. After deciding on the size, I could start the process of constructing the cabin.

Some of the materials I had on hand were left over from homes I had built over the years as a building contractor, including the six-by-six posts I used as supports for the floor joist system, and tongue and groove plywood for the subfloor. The hemlock lumber for the framing, including joists, studs, beams and rafters came from trees cut from our forest. Our logger had cut and the sawyer milled the trees in exchange for the use of our landing, an area cleared for stockpiling logs. He was logging the neighbors' property and needed an alternative route because endangered wood turtles were on the move across the logger's original exit path and landing. The state regulates access over migration areas while the turtles come out of hibernation and move ever so slowly to their breeding grounds which are usually a vernal pool in a low-lying area.

Up to this point the framing lumber had cost me nothing. A year earlier I had stacked the freshly cut lumber in our equipment shed with three one-inch-by-one-inch "stickers" between each successive layer to allow air flow for even drying. This job came quite naturally to me as this had been one of my tasks working in the family saw mill in my twenties. Unfortunately I was left with hearing loss from another job I had at the mill which involved removing the slabs and boards as they were sawn off the logs by the sawyer. I was positioned between a saw blade, five feet in diameter, whining in my left ear and a diesel power unit roaring in my right. Back then no one considered using hearing protection, so the damage was done.

The cabin's pine siding, flooring and interior trim also came from our trees. I gave the mill owner some logs from our forest in exchange for sawing our logs into boards which were then "stuck up" for two years until they were completely air dried. Then I took the entire pile to Kitza's Sawmill in Hadley and for seventy dollars I had them planed and ship-lapped for installation on the cabin.

Shiplapped siding

Thoreau used "refuse shingle" for the siding and roofing, and "two second-hand windows with glass" for which he paid $2.43. At a cost of $8.03½ he removed boards from a shanty that was previously occupied by chickens and the family it was purchased from. Keeping with Thoreau's philosophy of salvaging or finding the most economic options, I acquired the lumber for siding in trade. For my roof I used black three-tab asphalt shingles that I had purchased twenty-five years ago at a closeout price of thirty dollars for six square or 600 square feet, an amount which was more than enough for the cabin with the balance being used to reroof our chicken coop.

The ten by fifteen foot cabin does not have a conventional foundation but is supported by six pressure treated six inch by six inch posts. The cabin is situated on a bit of an incline; the low side sits on two foot posts, the upper sits on a six inch block with the back corner resting on bedrock with a pressure treated spacer between the joists and ledge. Ledges and rock outcroppings are quite plentiful here in New England, with an occasional "erratic" boulder, some six to eight feet high, deposited by the retreating glacier after the last ice age some 15,000 to 20,000 years ago.

Erratic "Tipping Rock" in Westhampton, Massachusetts

## "ERRATICS"

*Witness to generations of tall pine and mighty oak their lifespan,*
*one hundred years.*
*These sentinels of their woodland domain have not moved in*
*ten thousand years*
*Watched one hundred generations – birth, death: germination and regeneration.*
*— they have not moved —*
*The ground they stand upon has ebbed and flowed*
*like the sea in slow motion - imperceptible - erosion.*
*Dropped and left by a mile high crystal wall…created one snowflake at a time.*
*Wait ten years it appeared stationary … watch a lifetime.*
*Frozen water wall, like a bulldozer as wide as North America, scraped the terrain — everything in its path, nothing was sacred, nothing was spared…. end moraine. Then gave birth on New England earth, a multitude.*
*Slow retreat*
*These sentinels hailed from the north one mile, ten miles, one hundred, they will not reveal. Amongst the trees on the forest floor they stand – some in sight of each other, in groups or solitary, some of their kin in the meadow. Their southern sojourn took one…………hundred………. thousand………years, never to return.*
*They are very patient*
*Water entered fissures, froze, divided, split. One sentinel became two…. or more. Some teeter upon others, tipping rock begs. If they topple they may move a few feet – they are happy where they land….witnessing. Another ice age may wipe the slate clean…start all over again, advance and retreat, cycle upon timeless cycle.*

John Clapp

Since there was no electricity at the site, all lumber was calculated and cut at the house and carried out on the tractor. The framing took about a year, working part time with my son, Jarred, who helped when I needed an extra hand. Although we lacked electricity, I was aided with a gas actuated nail gun. (A small explosion in the cylinder of the gun drives a piston attached to a rod which drives a nail into the framing lumber. No need for an electric air compressor and gun.)

After the floor joists system was completed and a subfloor applied, we attached the five inch by five inch corner posts to the floor. One by one, we assembled the two-by-four stud walls on the floor, allowing for the door and window openings then lifted them into place between the posts. Next, we lifted the five-inch-square beams atop the posts and stud walls and in the center a single beam connecting front and back walls. To finish the framing, we nailed pre-cut rafters sixteen inches on center to the top of the wall on one end and to the ridge pole on the other.

By fall I was pushing to get the plywood on the exterior walls and get the roof on, which I accomplished with Jarred's help. Fall is the time of the year for the annual southern migration of Canada geese passing in V-formation overhead, and each year in my imagination their persistent honking was directed at me. They were reminding me with their laughter, "HONK-HONK-HONK, winter is coming and you don't have all your firewood cut yet, HONK-HONK." That year it was, "winter is coming and you don't have your roof on yet."

I had staging set up so we could reach the roof. I applied weathered ship-lapped pine boards on top of the rafters. From the inside, the rafters were left exposed giving the ceiling an authentic look. Only a single layer of tar paper on the roof kept the weather out that first winter. Eventually, I applied two inch by two inch sleepers or spacers directly over the two-inch-by six-inch rafters and ceiling boards (which created a void that allowed me to install two inch rigid foam insulation between the two-inch-by two-inch sleepers). I applied five-eighths-inch plywood over everything.

The last piece of plywood at the top was just out of my comfortable reach, not being as agile as I used to be. Seeing my struggle, my son, who was nineteen years old at the time, offered to climb to the top of the roof to secure the final piece with the nail gun. In that moment, it felt to me like a rite of passage for Jarred, a passing of the torch, or in this case, nail gun. I happily and gracefully accepted his help without feeling too old and accepted the limitations of a 65 year old. In turn, Jarred was sensitive enough to take on the task without any sense of superiority, he was just happy to help his Dad. It was a point in my life when that transition of power could comfortably happen. When I told him I couldn't have done it without him, it was true and heartfelt.

*Chapter Five*

# *Finishing the Cabin: The Story of a Door*

The next year I busied myself with finishing the cabin, insulating the walls and covering them with sheetrock. I applied sheetrock compound overall and left it with a slightly uneven affect to create the appearance of plaster. I painted the interior walls with an exterior paint the color of plaster. I chose exterior paint to better withstand the extremes of hot and cold and which inhibited condensation from penetrating the softer finish of the sheetrock. For the siding and roof shingles, I brought the generator and compressor and appropriate air guns to help with the nailing, cutting the time by eighty percent over nailing by hand. I had cut the siding to length and pre-stained the pieces at the house.

The front door is a reproduction of the door on the "Indian House" in Deerfield, Massachusetts, made famous by the raid in 1704. The attack on Deerfield by more than three hundred French soldiers and Indian warriors was a well-planned attempt to kidnap as many people as possible and take them back to Canada. Their goal was for the hostages to either be ransomed back to their families, or to be adopted by the French or Indian families. The native population had been drastically diminished due to European diseases to which the Indians had no immunity; by 1700 their population had been reduced by ninety percent.

The raid was conducted by the French, in cooperation with the Abenaki, Huron, Penacook, Iroquois of the Mountain and Mohawk Indians. The villagers were protected by a palisade which enclosed the majority of the houses, but the snow had drifted so high that the raiding party was able to breach the stockade wall allowing them to open the main gate from within. The attackers killed 50 people and burned eight homes. They chopped a hole through the door of the home of John Sheldon, and the attackers randomly shot their muskets through the freshly made hole in the door, killing Mrs. Sheldon. Sheldon's three year old daughter was also killed because they believed she couldn't survive the long trip to Canada. Their thinking was simple: better to kill prior to the trip those who would suffer and die from exposure. The young and weak would slow them on their journey home and many did die from exposure. Those that could not keep up were killed on the spot with a "clonk" to the head. This seems rather brutal but no more ruthless than the attacks by the English on the Native population who were rightfully protecting their homeland.

The raiding party kidnapped as many of the villagers as they could manage. A total of 112 men, women and children, including the rest of the inhabitants of the Sheldon household, were taken on foot to Canada, a long and grueling journey of 300 miles that took 27 days in the dead of winter. Of the 112 kidnapped, 21 died on route and 57 were eventually returned. Many of the captives chose to stay with their adopted families and not return to their strict Puritan religion and difficult lifestyle back in Deerfield.

In the summer of 2014 my wife and I went to "Plimoth Plantation" where we spent most of our time at the Native American encampment. This village is a reproduction of a Wampanoag settlement with Native Americans representing the Native people past and present, unlike the English Settlement where they portrayed the "Pilgrims" seven years after they arrived and only spoke in character from that period. The Native Americans spoke in present day language and demonstrated traditional crafts and explained the lifestyles of both early and present native people.

We were met at the entrance to the village by a man outfitted in traditional garb and seated in an electric wheelchair, which he explained was the result of having had polio. We struck up a conversation with him and I told him about Mary, an ancestor of mine who was taken to Canada by the French and Native People. She was first taken to *Kahnawake*, the Mohawk Village across the river from Montreal, and was then sent to an Abenaki village. His response was, "Those were my people!" He shared with us that he was an Abenaki from Odanak, or St. Francis, in Quebec, the very community in which Mary lived for three years. After three hundred years, we were talking to a descendent of the people who had not only kidnapped, but cared for Mary, who would become my fifth-great-grandmother!

Our conversation led to a mutual acknowledgement that both cultures were responsible for numerous bad deeds. Both cultures were responding to the pressures of that time period; the English needed land and destroyed the lives of many Native Americans in the process, and the Native people acted out of revenge for being displaced, often with brutal attacks on the English. It was so moving that we could be discussing the horror that each culture perpetrated on the other, with understanding and without animosity, that I was overcome with emotion and nearly in tears after our half-hour conversation. In his tribe he was honored by being the holder of the ceremonial pipe. He knew much about the 1704 Raid on Deerfield, especially from the perspective of the Abenaki. I felt honored to be in his presence.

On the night of the attack, the "Old Indian House," as the Sheldon house came to be known, was inhabited by many, including John Sheldon's daughter Mary and her four siblings and a sister in law, Hannah, three of whom, along with Mary, were among those taken to Canada. After three years they were ransomed back to their father. Up until that point, Sheldon believed his children were all dead until he received a letter from a man who had been part of the household with one of his daughters.

I pray give my kind love to Landlord Shelden and tel Him that i am sorry for all e his Los. I doe in these few Lins Doe Showe youe that god Has shone yo grat kindness and marcy In carrying youre Daighter Hanna and mary in pertickeler through so grat a iorney far beiend my expecttations noing How Lame thay war; the Rest of yore children are with the Indians Rememberrance lives near cabect Hannah doe Lives with the frenc In the same house i doe.

Collection of Deerfield Museums, Deerfield Massachusetts

Above is the letter sent to John Sheldon informing him that his children were indeed alive, despite being told a year prior that they were no longer alive.

On Mary's return (she was now eighteen) she found that her fiancé, Jonathan, had given her up for dead and had married someone else. Within a year she married Samuel Clapp, my fifth great-grandfather. During their life together in Northampton, Mary's adopted Abenaki mother for years would travel the three hundred miles from Canada to spend the summers with her, a testament to the bond they had developed. It appeared the visits may have been timed for the harvest; "They always came when Clapp's corn was green, and would devour it in great quantities, roasting the ears at a fire under an apple tree." Interestingly, in 1761 Samuel died as well as the wife of Mary's fiancé from years past. Mary, at 75, and Jonathan, 80, married, having one year together before Mary died, while Jonathan died three years later.

I found it fitting to build a replica of the Sheldon door for my cabin. As it turned out, the construction of this door was similar to Thoreau's. The original door on John Sheldon's house was designed to withstand an Indian attack, as the village had been raided before. He used two layers of oak, the first layer perpendicular to the second with ship-lapped edges to make the door impervious to weather. Unfortunately, it proved inadequate against a persistent tomahawk. (Folklore claims it was a tomahawk but I would bet it was a European metal ax that cut through the two-inch solid oak door.) They actually gained entrance through a less fortified back door. The original front door survived and can be seen at the Memorial Hall Museum at Historic Deerfield.

For my door I used pine cut from our land, since oak would be much stronger than I needed and I did not expect any raiding parties, although we are under attack by the Wooly Adelgid and the Asian

Long Horned beetle, their wrath directed upon our hemlock and maple trees. The construction of my door includes two vertical ship-lap boards sixteen inches wide by one-inch thick. The inside layer has six horizontal boards, and I had all the boards sandblasted to give the door a weather-beaten appearance. The two layers were nailed together with reproduction hand-cut, rosehead nails to add to the authenticity. These nails were also used on the interior trim and wide pine floor boards. The door latch and strap hinges were hand forged by the blacksmith shop in the neighboring town of Williamsburg. The weakest point of a house is the door sill because it takes the most abuse and is stepped on more than any other spot. Wet snow and rain add to its susceptibility to rot, and a wooden door sill is the first to go. For my sill, I chose a species of wood that will perhaps outlast the rest of the building: Ipe or Brazilian Walnut is a dense hardwood that is extremely resistant to moisture and wear. With the plan of fabricating my own sill, I purchased one three-feet by eight-inch by two-inch plank of ipe at a cost of sixty dollars, double the historical cost of Thoreau's entire cabin.

Henry spent $28.12½ in all for his cabin; everything else was salvaged, save the labor it took to remove the structures he was dismantling. My final out-of-pocket costs were $1,772.78. A quick comparison of the dollar value in 1845, compared to present day value, revealed that one dollar then would be worth approximately thirty dollars today, so in 1845 dollar value I would have spent $60, or about double the cost of Henry's cabin. This was still an impressive savings; if my cabin had been built for a customer I would put the value at $25,000. On the next page are the comparable materials for each cabin.

Before building his cabin, Henry had helped his father construct their family home on Texas Street (now Belknap Street) in Concord. Henry made much of the furniture for his cabin and was indeed resourceful here as in most of his endeavors. The furniture for my cabin is a reflection of some of Thoreau's choices, including a bed, a desk and three chairs. Henry's three chairs represented to him, "one for solitude, two for friendship and three for society." His bed, desk, chairs and surveying equipment survive and are on display in the Concord Museum.

| My Costs | | Henry's Costs | |
|---|---|---|---|
| Permit | $25.00 | Boards (mostly shanty boards) | $8.03 ½ |
| Plywood | $517.54 | Refuse shingles for roof and sides | $4.00 |
| Drip edge | $47.81 | Laths | $1.25 |
| Planing and shiplap | $70.00 | | |
| Roofing | $30.00 | | |
| Rigid foam insulation | $218.88 | 2 second hand windows with glass | $2.43 |
| Tar paper | $28.44 | 1,000 old brick | $4.00 |
| Cut nails | $109.72 | Nails | $3.90 |
| Sheetrock | $111.38 | 2 casks of lime (that was high) | $2.40 |
| Stovepipe | $5.91 | Hair (more than I needed) | $0.31 |
| Fiberglass insulation | $125.87 | Mantle-tree iron | $0.15 |
| Door hardware (Williamsburg Blacksmith) | $108.51 | Hinges and screws | $0.14 |
| Ipe door sill | $61.41 | Latch | $0.10 |
| Stain | $42.31 | Chalk | $0.01 |
| Sandblasting front door | $95.00 | Transportation (I carried a good part on my back) | $1.40 |
| Sandblasting stove | $100.00 | | |
| Stove heat paint | $75.00 | | |
| Total | $1772.78 | In all | $28.12 ½ |

Of the furniture in my cabin, the one piece I built myself was a wood box for storing fire wood. I had constructed it years earlier when I made Shaker furniture reproductions to sell at shops and craft fairs. The wood box idea came from a design book of early Shaker furniture that I would refer to and select pieces I thought would be both challenging to build and that would sell. Items such as peg-boards, candle sconces and small hanging cabinets and mirrors were my "bread and butter" items, and larger cabinets, writing desks and wood boxes sold occasionally. This particular box never sold, which allowed me to use it at the cabin as well as in every other wood-heated home I've lived in since. With its rich patina, dovetailed top and well-worn appearance it can pass as an original.

Most of the lumber I used in making my Shaker pieces came from our saw mill where I was able to hand-pick clear pine boards, some over sixteen inches wide. I would store these boards in the attic of my 1790 Cape in Westhampton which doubled as my woodworking shop where I covered the wall over the work bench with a large collection of antique hand tools. I have always enjoyed woodworking, finding it both relaxing and satisfying, and I would much rather listen to the "zhhh zhhh zhhh" of a back saw while cutting dovetail joints than the loud whirr of an electric router. Smoothing the edge of a board with the subtle "vvvvvvvit" sound of a hand plane while peeling off a paper-thin ribbon of wood in a continuous tight curl is superior to using its electric counterpart.

Previous to setting up the shop, my friend and then house-mate, Paul, himself a master cabinetmaker, introduced me to the resident woodworker at the Hancock Shaker Village in Hancock, Massachusetts. Joel was about to teach a class in joinery, which I decided to attend.

The workshop was held at the reconstructed Eastfield Village in New York State established by Don Carpentier, a preservationist who had a passion for conserving nineteenth-century crafts and structures. Weeklong classes were offered in various trades including blacksmithing, tinsmithing, shoemaking and woodworking. The instructors were masters of their respective trade, and taught their students with the backdrop of an authentic 1840s settlement that included a tavern, print shop, blacksmith shop, cabinet shop, church and doctor's office. All twenty structures had been salvaged from the surrounding area and were moved to the site located in the middle of a fourteen-acre wood lot, and all were situated around a grassy central common.

My class was held at the church, minus the pews where the only utterances of "Jesus" or "God" were made in vain after a misplaced blow of a mallet. There were ten or twelve other students in my class, and we learned to cut both open and blind dovetail joints, and the mortise and tenon joints used in stile and rail construction of paneled cabinet doors, all with traditional hand tools. We also were shown the proper way to sharpen chisels and planer blades by hand on an oil stone, and how to put on a finished edge by "stropping" them on a piece of leather.

Each craft was taught in one of the designated buildings, but at meal time we would all head for the tavern for a hearth-cooked meal including fresh bread from a traditional Dutch oven. There was no phone or electricity, and water had to be hand pumped from a well. The call of nature would have to be accomplished at the privy, and on a hot day you had no trouble finding it. All lighting was with candles, and participants were asked to bring their own supply. I truly felt I was visiting a country hamlet in 1840.

And I felt right at home. At the time I lived in and was restoring a 1790 Cape with back-to-back Rumford fireplaces. The one in the kitchen had a crane that could swing out, enabling you to hang a cast iron pot or kettle to cook stew or heat water over the fire. I made good use of the beehive bake-oven that was located next to the fireplace. I would build a fire in the morning and by afternoon I pulled out the ashes and put in pans of freshly kneaded bread dough. I would make multiple loaves so we could enjoy them through the week. After the bread was taken out I would take advantage of the remaining heat by popping in and heating up a casserole for supper.

One cold winter night I turned the heat off as part of an experiment. I wanted to experience what the original family of this house would have had to do to stay warm. I banked up a load of firewood in

the Rumford fireplace, setting a soapstone heater before the blazing fire. As we got ready for bed, I grabbed the handle of the hot soapstone and ran it between the sheets making the bed quite toasty. This was a nightly ritual in colonial America until woodstoves became available. I can say that we were able to stay warm throughout the night with the aid of a few extra blankets, although by morning with the fire out it was cold, making it difficult to get out of bed. The experience certainly helped me appreciate what our ancestors had to endure.

Upon my return home from the joinery workshop, in addition to my full time carpentry job building log houses, I now spent countless hours at my new craft turning out peg boards, candle sconces, wood boxes and other assorted small pieces until I had enough inventory to join the craft fair circuit. On one of my first days back on the job, Barr, for whom I had worked for only a short time, gently urged me to speed it up after taking what he thought was an excessive amount of time installing window trim on the new home we were building. "We're not making Shaker furniture here, John," he chided.

*Chapter Six*

# *Ides of March, 2014*

In mid-March I had the opportunity to spend my first overnight at the cabin. Our bed and breakfast guests had planned to visit a local "sugar shack" so I didn't have to be up early to make and serve them breakfast. It was a full moon and bright enough to make my way up the path without a flashlight. I started a fire in the pot-bellied stove and settled in for the night. After a meal of Chinese take-out and a quick read from *Walden; One Hundred Years After Thoreau,* a poetry book written by our friend Donald, I was ready for bed.

My woodstove is a vintage Sears and Roebuck model given to us by our friends Ed and Jody twenty years ago. I loaded the stove for the night, not knowing how soon it would burn through the full load, but I assumed I would be refilling it part-way through the night. To my horror, it burned through quickly, even though all the dampers were shut. Within an hour it was over one hundred degrees in the cabin, despite my having opened the windows, and the bottom of the stove was glowing red hot. There was simply no way to shut it down. I got no sleep for the first hour. The combination of sweating profusely from the excess heat and the cold wind coming in from outside made for a truly unpleasant first stay. I decided to forego another runaway fire and accepted the fact that I would sleep better in the cold.

I had winter-camped in the past when it was ten degrees above zero, so I figured that an insulated cabin with no heat had to be warmer than an exposed nylon tent. I doubled up the quilt and pulled a small woven rug over me. This rug was made by the same friend who gave us the woodstove, so it seems that Ed was destined to keep me warm one way or another. I easily survived the change from more than one hundred degrees to a temperature of forty degrees which it was when I got up the next morning; outside it was twenty degrees. I decided to wait until spring for the next attempt.

Although winter camping was always a challenge, I preferred it to any other season, for several reasons: I had the place to myself, there were no bugs, and I liked the satisfaction of knowing that I was able to survive it. With a sleeping bag good for minus ten degrees, I knew I would always be toasty. The worst part was preparing food outside on a campstove without gloves. Even a slight breeze created a ten below wind chill. I had learned a few tricks to stay warmer in frigid weather, like bringing my boots into the sleeping bag so they wouldn't be frozen in the morning. Also, even though it seems counter-intuitive, a cold drink of water in the middle of the night would warm your core, but you would have to remember to insulate your canteen to keep the water from freezing.

My past experience with winter camping often took place atop Mt. Negus in Rowe, Massachusetts and was always spectacular, with Mt. Monadnock to the northeast and Mt. Greylock to the west. The Deerfield River meanders through the valley at the foot of the mountain, and the railroad tracks parallel the river. On a crisp night I could hear the rumble of the train from miles away; the whistle piercing the stillness of the night. As the train grew closer the sound of the engine would roll up the side of the mountain. At the base of the mountain the train would sound like it was passing right outside the tent, a reminder that, even though you were miles from any house, at an altitude of 1773 feet, civilization was not far away. Perhaps this sound was similar to Thoreau's experience living by Walden Pond, frozen in winter, with railroad tracks just across the pond.

With hypothermia and frostbite a real concern, learning how to properly dress for camping in extremely cold weather is of the utmost importance. Polar fleece, Gore Tex and polypropylene were just becoming popular for winter gear when I started winter camping. These clothes, with proper layering, promotes wicking (migration of moisture to the outer layers), resulting in drier layers next to your skin, helping to keep you quite warm. We lived in Shelburne Falls, Massachusetts, in the 1990s and one of my favorite pastimes was to suit up in these clothes and go for a very comfortable winter walk around town while the outside temperature was well below zero. Again, no one was outside and I had the streets to myself.

*Chapter Seven*

# *Mt. Tom and the New Village of Northampton*

In the 1630s, twenty years before Northampton, or Nonotuck as it was then called, was settled, the nearby mountain was simply called "The Great Mountain." Eventually it was renamed Mount Tom after Thomas Rowland who was exploring the wilds west of Springfield which was then the most westerly village in Massachusetts.

Rowland, along with his partner, Elizur Holyoke, for whom Mount Holyoke was named, were looking for land to settle, as the English expanded deeper into the territory. Nonotuck had rich soil for farming and rivers for water power and navigation. The land was procured by Colonel John Pynchon from the Nonotuck Indians. Pynchon had a monopoly on trade and land acquisition in western Massachusetts, which made him one of the wealthiest and most powerful men in the area, and was the "go to" man for negotiations with the native people. Chickwallop, with other Nonotuck chiefs, accepted "one hundred fathoms of wampum and ten skins" in trade for 64,000 acres of prime farming, trapping, fishing, and hunting land that would become known as part of the "Pioneer Valley." By 1654, settlers or "planters" as they were then called, arrived and the new town of Northampton was divided into home lots which were given to families who agreed that they would remain for at least two years.

My earliest ancestor in this country, Captain Roger Clap, (back then spelled with only one "p") arrived in New England from Devon, England in 1630 and helped settle Dorchester, Massachusetts. In appreciation for Roger's service to town and state, including his stint as Captain of the militia and Commander of the troops at The Castle, the earliest fort in Boston Harbor, he was awarded a large tract of land in Northampton. This land extended from South Street to the present border of Easthampton.

Roger lived the remainder of his life in Boston and passed on the Northampton land to his children (he had thirteen children, seven of whom lived to adulthood). His son, Supply Clap, was killed at the age of twenty-six: "he hath one of his eyes shot out, and a piece of his skull taken away, by the accidental firing of a gun, as he was going a fowling." Supply had been an officer at the fort his father commanded. Supply had brothers and sisters with equally unusual names such as Preserved, Experience, Thanks, Desire, Unite, Waitstill, Hopestill and Wait. When Wait was baptized, we learn from James Blake who was an early historian and close friend of Roger's, her father explained "that the reason he called her Wait was because he believed the reign of the anti-Christ would be soon be over...thinking that she might live to see the day."

Roger's son Preserved, my direct ancestor, received four acres in Northampton in 1671, and he became a prominent citizen in both church and town government. James Blake wrote that Preserved "was a great blessing to the town." Serving as Captain in the military, he was opposed to the local militia officers being chosen by John Pynchon and felt that they should be picked by those who would be serving under them. Lieutenant John King, along with Preserved and Medad Pomeroy, organized a mutiny and no longer obeyed Pynchon's orders; and apparently, they were supported by the majority of people in town. Pynchon's military officers referred to the three men as "hard-drinking, quarrelsome malcontents," but the resistance served its purpose and they were granted, or established their own authority to choose their own officers. Preserved served in the militia for over twenty years and rose to rank of Captain and fought in both the Turners Falls battle and in King William's War. Preserved had lost his home during a raid against the southern part of Northampton when the natives set it ablaze along with three other homes. Preserved died in Northampton in 1720 at 77 years of age. By the 1850s the descendants of Roger who received the Northampton land had built many homes along South Street. A map published in 1856 showed sixteen Clapps on a half mile stretch, one third the total of all residents on that street.

Preserved's son Samuel was born in Northampton in 1677 and later married Mary Sheldon who was taken to Canada after the raid on Deerfield in 1704. Samuel and Mary lived on South Street, their property being later donated by one of their descendants to create the Lathrop Retirement home.

View from Mt. Tom towards the cabin

*Chapter Eight*

# *A la mode for the Abode*

To top off the cabin, I installed a single 110-watt solar panel which I had salvaged from my sister's house. I built a one foot by two foot pine box in which I placed two six-volt deep cycle batteries for storage and a charge controller that allows the batteries to be fully charged without over-charging. The system produces enough electricity for a single twenty-watt DC light bulb, and a DC outlet for charging a laptop. "Me thinks" this would have met with the approval of Thoreau.

My entire family home is similarly powered by a two-kilowatt (or 2000 watt) solar array with a bank of 36 six-volt batteries for storage. It supplies electricity for the house, farm and three guest rooms at our bed and breakfast. We are independent from the electric company, and on sunny days we have electricity to spare. After a few cloudy days, however, we may have to start the back-up generator for an hour or two to recharge the batteries. This process holds us until the next sunny day.

While replacing the batteries every eight to ten years is costly at $150 each, we have not had an electric bill in sixteen years. The initial outlay of $10,000 for the entire system was equal to the cost of bringing electric cables back from the poles at the road, a distance of a quarter of a mile. The decision was simple; hook up to the grid and pay them one hundred dollars a month or more for as long as we live, or invest in a photovoltaic system and never see another electric bill. The real benefit is reducing our carbon footprint. Our system is 120 volts since we have an inverter that ramps up the 24-volt direct current battery power to 120 volts, and changes direct current to alternating current (AC) which is typical in conventional homes.

While the photovoltaic system seems quite simple, the deeper workings are extraordinary. It takes particles of light (photons) eight minutes to travel from the sun at 186,000 miles per second to reach earth and the solar panels. A photon collides with an electron of an atom in the silicon absorbing panel, knocking the electron out of its orbit into a positive receiving "hole" in the back of the silicon of the solar panel, which in turn creates an extremely small positive charge and is "collected" by a very fine grid which can be seen under the glass of the panel. This charge flows along with billions of others to create a current that is carried to the battery bank by wires and is stored until needed. In its entirety, this is a much more extraordinary process than my very basic explanation implies. Henry would definitely give this a nod.

*Chapter Nine*

# *A Shack up in the Woods: A Tribute to Jack*

In 1975, my friend and mentor Jack and I built a cabin on a 36-acre woodlot I owned and where I had planned to build a full-sized house one day. Our original plan was to construct a lean-to where we could camp out, but it quickly evolved into a ten foot by ten foot cabin. My motivation for this cabin was a desire to have a getaway where I could be out in the woods and enjoy nature. We picked a spot on a side hill in the middle of that woodlot in Westhampton, Massachusetts. Back then, I only had a vague knowledge of Thoreau and no idea what his philosophy on transcendentalism was.

I knew of Jack in my junior high school years. He was a few years ahead of me and not in my peer group, but was part of the Leeds gang, a group of semi-hoodlums from a neighboring town, with a reputation for being on the wild side. One perhaps apocryphal story circulated about how they fitted a homemade motorized vehicle with wheels from a railroad car. This allowed them to rip along the tracks, out of reach of the police, perhaps being pursued after blowing up a mail box with a cherry bomb or maybe for stealing hubcaps. The extent of my own vandalism was to place a penny on the tracks and wait for the train to flatten it. If I wanted to ratchet it up I would use a nickel. I always looked up to them, and even though their antics were frowned upon by most, they were "too cool" in my eyes. I was just a "hayseed," a derogatory term for farm kids back then, and I wished I could be more like them. Jack, in my eyes, was elevated to a near god.

After a stint in the army, Jack enrolled in a drafting class at the trade school where I was attending a four-year course in agriculture.

I had no interest in farming, but the decision had been made by my father. He expected I would become a farmer and carry on the family tradition which was started by my great-great grandfather in 1826. Myself, I hated being in "aggie."

The conflict with my father about becoming a farmer entered my dream life at an early age. I started having dreams about being chased by a bull around ten or twelve years of age and they continued through early adulthood. In reality we kept a young bull as a stud but in these recurring dreams it was fully mature with large horns and always with a ring in its nose. (In real life bulls would be fitted with a ring and with a twist one could control their aggressive behavior.) In my dream, when caught in an open meadow by the large bull, it would thunder after me snorting its disapproval at my intruding on its territory. I could always keep a few steps ahead of him and at the last second I would duck under the barbed wire fence avoiding being gored by its horns. I always seemed to manage to get away but as these dreams progressed, the bull got cagier. With an almost human ability, it would pursue me no matter where I would hide. In a later dream, I picked a place I thought it could not follow. I ran into the house and up the back stairs to my bedroom, only to find it had developed the ability to climb stairs. In yet another dream I scampered up into our hay mow only to find it could easily negotiate the steeply stacked bales of hay. I simply could not get away.

*I bought this print at the Louvre gift shop well after the dream series concluded. I was struck by how much the image fit the dreams. No one could tell me the artist's name.*

The bull was always intimidating in its pursuit, although I don't ever remember it actually catching up with me; it just terrified me with its persistent chase. As I got older, I developed ways to take control, and in one dream the bull cornered me in the paddock and instead of attempting to get away, I turned on the bull, grabbing it by the horns and twisting its head to the ground, much like a cowboy at a rodeo. I would then run away in fear.

The last significant bull dream occurred while I was in my late twenties. This time the bull found me in the middle of an open field and instead of chasing me, it ran circles around me perhaps thirty feet away. It seemed to be sizing me up for an attack. After a number of passes the bull transformed into a human form resembling Chairman Mao, who continued to circle, only now at a slower pace. I'm not sure what my association with Mao would have been other than an early interest in everything "Oriental" although I did have a copy of his *Little Red Book* in my library. He then began throwing ninja stars at me which I was able to avoid until one struck me, sticking into my hip. I pulled it out and threw it back at him, the star finding its mark, striking his head, killing him. I had at last won the battle with the bull.

For years I would occasionally have dreams of the bull, reminding me that he was still lurking just beneath the surface of my subconscious. The bull did not directly represent my father, but was more about my early relationship with him and about my struggle to find my own identity separate from my early self-image as a farm kid.

After spending four years in the agricultural department my only consolation was that my dad allowed me to attend a two-year course in the auto body department, part of the Smith Vocational School I had graduated from. With the exception of a few months working in an auto body shop, I really only used those skills to fix up and paint my '55 and '57 Chevy hot-rods over the years.

One year, prior to winter setting in, I removed the motor from the '57 Chevy and with help from a friend, carried it "down cellar" in my father's house for a rebuild as well as to "hop it up" with Jahns racing pistons, an Iskenderian high lift cam, and a Mallory dual point distributor along with an Edelbrock duel-carb aluminum manifold and twin Holly four barrel carburetors. In the spring after the motor

was completely rebuilt, I would haul it out of the cellar and install the 301-cubic-inch motor (it was a stock 283 bored out to a 301) into my freshly painted Chevy. The final parts to be installed were a set of exhaust headers, each consisting of a single pipe from each exhaust port, all four exiting into a four-inch collector which connected to a glasspack muffler. While racing, the muffler would be disconnected and was bolted away from the header allowing for unrestricted flow of exhaust resulting in more horsepower.

I couldn't wait to get to the race track to test it out so, on one warm, sunny Sunday afternoon, with my family peacefully resting after morning church service, I had to try it out. Firing it up without the mufflers attached was deafening, and of course I could not stop myself from squealing the tires and racing down the street with a cloud of tire smoke billowing from behind. I should have just kept driving. On my return home my father was waiting on the front piazza with his arms folded in front of him and I knew I was in for the scolding of my life. My father never swore and he didn't this time but in no uncertain terms he told me if I ever tried that again he would take away not only my license, but my car as well. He told me the noise rattled every window in the house and what was I trying to do, give him a heart attack? What the hell was I thinking? I guess in my own way I was telling him I'd rather be a gearhead than a farmer. My mother had once remarked to a cousin that cars were my "first love" and after that episode she probably hoped that the romance would end sooner than later.

This was a great distraction from farm life and helped me on my way to "coolness," as hot-rods and cruising the burger joints was the "in" thing to do back in the late '60s. There were many Sundays that I would arrive late for evening milking after spending the day at the drag races competing on the quarter-mile track at Lebanon Valley Speedway in New York State. This diversion helped me to disconnect from the family farming operation. Ironically, thirty years later, I was once again farming. But this time there were no cows to milk. Instead, in 2000 my wife and I started a farm raising llamas, emus, goats, chickens, peacocks, and a miniature donkey. The only thing that remained the same was haying and shoveling manure; the ins and outs of farm animals.

Jack seemed to always be on the periphery, in and out of my life. The next thing I know he was off to UMass where, on the G. I. Bill, he received an M.F.A. in painting. He was always part of the "in crowd" popular with the women with his long hair and full mustache, but now he was an "artist." Our paths crossed again in the early '70s, when Fritz (a mutual friend) suggested that I ask Jack for advice on the proper way to germinate pot seeds. I wanted to grow my own. I ran into him that fall at the Three County Fair in Northampton where he proceeded to instruct me in the propagation of "weed." As a result of our mutual interest, we became fast friends.

After leaving the farm in 1973, I purchased the woodlot where we eventually decided to build the cabin. The cabin was not the typical four walls and a roof, which, if left to my own devices, it would have been. I had deferred to Jack's design after he commented that I didn't have an aesthetic bone in my body. Back then, it was probably true. With Jack's artistic sensibility, it turned out quite stylish; with a sleeping loft, arched window and a porch where we could sit and contemplate nature.

The cabin sported a unique structural design, that incorporated a cross-brace system using three-inch by five-inch timbers attached to the corner posts on each wall that formed a large "X" with a half lap joint where they intersected. This created a strong lateral support system that doubled as a nailing surface for the siding, as there was no stud wall or plywood. The corner posts, joist supports and joists were all cut from five inches in diameter trees that we cleared from the site. The balance of the building materials for the cabin was salvaged, and the pine for the board and batten siding came from my family's sawmill.

At one point in the construction we needed to use my truck to pick up some supplies at Jack's house in Northampton. This truck was a 1950 Ford flatbed that I only used to haul firewood out of the woods. It did not have a current inspection sticker as the brakes were bad thanks to a slow leak in the line. On many occasions after draining the master cylinder reservoir of brake fluid as a result of the leak, I would have to rely on the emergency brake to bring the truck to a stop. Our solution to the inspection problem was to make up our own version of a sticker. We took an empty pack of Zig-Zag rolling papers and unfolded it. Opened, it was the approximate size and shape of the stickers placed on your windshield at the inspection station. Additionally it was the same red color of the current legal sticker back then. We taped it to the windshield and from a distance no one was the wiser. All we had to do was avoid being stopped by the cops for a broken tail light or for speeding. With Zig-Zag man as our co-pilot we made it into town and back without incident; the rolling paper caper was a success.

Being a couple of outlaws (at least in our own minds) and the fact that Jack's surname was Judge it was only appropriate to use a large arched window that had been salvaged from the Hampshire County Courthouse, which became the focal point of the cabin. A table, chairs, storage cabinet, a bed, a foam mattress in the loft, a well-worn oriental rug and a wood stove completed the nicely appointed interior. It turned out to be rustic but elegant, in a hippie sort of way. We placed a prominent hand-painted sign at the entrance of the woodlot that stated "NO TRESPASSING: VIOLATORS WILL BE PERSECUTED TO THE FULLEST EXTENT OF OUR INSANITY!!!" In our minds we thought this was clever, but in reality it was not particularly effective. One "trespasser" upon finding the cabin, proceeded to inform the authorities of our illegal shack. It seemed I had "forgotten" to obtain the appropriate building permit.

Jack and I enjoyed many years of drunk and disorderly conduct at the shack. For instance, after a barely memorable Halloween party, we stumbled our way up to the cabin to sleep it off, with Jack's wife and a friend of mine, dressed as a cat burglar, in tow. Ironically my costume had been a police officer's uniform. I had borrowed it from my housemate and friend Zippy, a town cop. But that's a story for another time. He did not ask for an explanation as to why the uniform was covered with dirt upon its return, as part of the climb up the hill to the cabin was done on all fours.

Our fine dining included steak readily available from my freezer which was liberally stocked after I bought a side of beef from a local farm. We would cook it in a cast iron skillet on top of the wood stove. Brookies and rainbow trout that we caught fresh from Marble brook just down the road were also on the menu. We ate like kings.

One year in mid-winter, I decided to spend two weeks at the cabin by myself. I had two goals in mind; to cut some tall pines as part of a selected logging operation of clearing a house site to be built on in the future, and to avoid the influences that kept me drinking beer. It was time for a change. Unfortunately, I came down with the flu and could only work on the latter, but I was determined to stay the full two weeks.

The road to the cabin was not plowed, so every few days I would walk the mile back to the main road where I parked my car and drive back home to get more food. Many nights during my stay, I would go out to the porch and enjoy the moon and stars. The air was frigid, with temperatures in the low twenties. The only sound was the snap of the frozen white birch trees when a gentle breeze would sway them. Eventually the crackling fire in the wood stove would draw me back inside.

One day during my extended stay I heard someone calling my name as they trudged up the snow-covered path to the cabin. Not being accustomed to visitors, I was a bit surprised, but having had no human contact for days, I was up for a little company. By the time the person reached the porch I recognized the petite woman as Jack's wife bundled against the cold looking like an Eskimo. She had hiked the long path from the main road bearing gifts, a plate of home-baked cookies. I must have looked like a mountain man; unshaven, disheveled with the same clothes I had worn for days, my shoulder-length hair tied in two pony tails. I guess I'm describing most hippies from that time. I was thankful for the visit and the cookies were much appreciated.

After the split from my first wife, Jack, his wife Helen, and I became inseparable spending many a night eating at Joe's Pizza and drinking pitchers of draft beer. Then we would head to their apartment, which was conveniently located across the street, for some Late Night TV with Johnny Carson.

Eventually, I sold the woodlot, as it did not have enough frontage to build a home and the town refused to grant me a variance on a non-conforming lot which meant that I could not build. My sister bought the land, as her property was contiguous with mine. (I'm sure she did not miss our cars passing by her side yard at two o'clock in the morning.)

Jack was the first friend I had outside of my neighbors, cousins and the school chums I had grown up with. He introduced me to books written by authors such as Carlos Castaneda, Kurt Vonnegut, George Orwell and Saul Bellow, staples in any good library of a counter-culture hippie.

On a warm summer evening we would meet, me on my Harley chopper and Jack on his borrowed Triumph, and we would ride through the countryside, the fringe of my leather jacket flapping in the wind, like a scene out of *Easy Rider*.

Jack moved to Brooklyn in the early 1980s to seek his fame and misfortune as an artist, but it wasn't meant to be. Jack was a hustler and was determined to do well at something, so he started Calhoun's, a small cabinet shop in Tribeca with a single partner. He had little money and sold his well-used Alfa Romeo to stake himself in the new venture. He and his business partner Sam, built this business into a large upscale custom cabinet shop. Jack eventually bought out

*Sam, John and Jack, Westhampton, Massachusetts*

Sam and continued to run the shop employing up to fifteen people. His clients included the Whitney Museum of Art, the Reverend Sun Myung Moon and the City of New York, building a judge's bench for the Court House. It wasn't the first time that Jack had to "approach the bench."

I arrived in Manhattan on one of my many visits to the City to spend a long weekend with Jack. I parked across the street from his shop and waited for him to return from an errand. I watched him round the corner and was struck by his determined stride and confident smile, looking like he owned a piece of New York, which he did. He was able to buy the first two floors of a co-op for his shop on Vestry Street where his neighbor, comedian David Letterman, owned the top floor.

Jack would make frequent pilgrimages back to the Pioneer Valley and his old stomping grounds. I had sold my house in Westhampton and was building a new home on the top of Chestnut Hill in Montague, Massachusetts. Jack would stop in and check on the progress from time to time and while I was adding the third floor he paid me a compliment on my design. It seemed I had been redeemed in his eyes from when I had no "aesthetic bones". Although there was a comment made about my house resembling the cabin which in a way it did, only on a much larger scale.

I lost Jack twenty years ago to a rare form of blood cancer. He was one in a long line of friends who died well before their time. I did not see Jack very often after the birth of our son. I suspected it was hard for him, as he was not in a stable relationship and did not see children in his immediate future, or perhaps he felt like he was intruding. I did not know about his cancer and had no contact with him in the year leading up to his death. I learned what happened from his distraught brother. In a bizarre phone call he said, "I have bad news, Jack got cancer. And it gets worse, he died." I miss Jack still, and cherish the great memories of the summer we spent together building the shack up in the woods.

# Chapter Ten

# *House on the Hill*

In 1984 I built my first full-sized home located in the hills of Montague, Massachusetts. The house was my own design and had many amenities, including an open floor plan on the first level with a cedar-lined sauna off the bathroom with a second door which led directly outside. After baking in the hot sauna for ten or fifteen minutes one had the option of a roll in the snow. Not for the faint of heart.

On the second floor there was a large balcony/library with a cathedral ceiling overlooking the kitchen. Located at the end of the kitchen was a six by eight foot entryway where I took advantage of the flat area above to create an inside arboretum/sitting room complete with lush green plants, crushed brick on the floor and a small arched cedar bridge connecting the balcony to the sitting area. With the high ceiling and full length arched topped window on the back wall it was certainly inviting. Off the balcony was a bathroom with a six foot jacuzzi in an alcove with a dividing wall supported on one end by a birch tree that I cut from the woods. The second-floor joist system consisted of exposed six-by-eight hemlock beams supporting four-by-six joists. Two-by-six tongue and grove southern yellow pine completed the floor system. The walls and ceiling were natural plaster and the entire house was trimmed with natural pine.

I don't believe Thoreau would have approved of this house with all the luxuries, although he would have appreciated the location. I chose a hilltop on Chestnut Hill Loop for its remoteness. My nearest neighbor was a half mile away and it being a loop or circular extension to the main road, no one used it unless they lived on the sparsely populated unpaved road. I did keep my expenses down by purchasing much of the materials from the "bargain barn" at the local lumber yard—items ordered by customers and never picked up, such as doors, windows, cabinets etc., which the yard heavily discounted. I would travel far and wide for the best deals, plus I did much of the labor myself and I sporadically hired friends to help.

I was fortunate to have my two closest friends as part of my crew which made the summer go by quickly. As well as being crew members, Tom and Ron had been my best men at Dee's and my wedding and I had stood up as best man at their weddings. With our shared irreverent sense of humor we all got along famously.

What made the house unique was the third floor which was just a single ten-by-twelve-foot room similar to a captain's watch or widow's walk on an old Victorian seacoast home. But the similarities stopped there. The room was a replica of a Japanese Tea House complete with a four and a half-mat tatami floor. Each mat measured three by six feet with a three-by-three-foot mat in the center creating a nine-foot-square floor bordered with four-inch cedar trim. The walls and ceiling were natural plaster that I left unpainted. In the front I installed a three foot in diameter round window and below, on a raised four-inch platform, was an eighteen-inch-wide solid cherry board the full width of the room. This would be for displaying flower arrangements with a scroll of calligraphy hung above. A large picture window in the rear provided a view of the thickly wooded back yard with an operating window on each side for cross-ventilation. Access to this room was gained through the second-floor bedroom. One had to pull out the wooden ladder which was hinged at the top, then climb seven feet, entering a three foot square opening that led to the "moon room." On occasion I would serve tea to guests in my third-story tea house but I used it mostly for yoga and meditation.

I had studied Japanese tea ceremony for years and found it complimentary to my Zen training. Serving ceremonial tea has its roots in Zen. In a traditional tea house the host would offer green tea to guests in a highly ritualized ceremony incorporating slow deliberate meditative moves. Guests would enter through a three foot square sliding door. Throughout history, the Samurai would leave their swords at the door upon entry, showing respect to the host and other guests. It also made them vulnerable, another sign of respect and trust. The act of bending down and sliding in on your knees is considered a symbol of respect, humbling yourself and demonstrating that guest and host are equals. The entire ceremony is accomplished while sitting on one's legs.

The serving of a cup of tea to one person could take as long as thirty minutes which would include a ritualized separate cleaning of the bowl and each bamboo utensil. A tea sweet would then be offered, followed by the preparation of a cup of green tea. Making the tea would involve scooping a small mound of powdered tea into the bowl, into which a ladle of boiling water would be added, then

using a multi-tined bamboo whisk, the contents would be whisked to a froth. The cup would be offered to the guest who would pause to appreciate the color and shape of the bowl before partaking of the tea. The guest would inquire about the poetic name of the particular bowl, each of which has its own story.

There are four concepts to be held in mind while partaking and serving tea; harmony, respect, purity and tranquility, which permeate all aspects of tea ceremony. To become a master at *Chanoyu,* or tea, you would spend years perfecting the form as well as studying the philosophy. With the great respect shown for nature and the flora and fauna it contains, all being a natural extension of tea ceremony, I believe Thoreau would have appreciated it. The Japanese word *wabi,* which roughly translates to "rustic simplicity," is used to describe the simple design of the tea utensils, including *raku* tea bowls or *chawan,* hand-made of clay, *chasen* or tea whisk, *chashaku* or tea scoop, and *hishaku* or ladle for dipping hot water for making tea, all hand-made from bamboo. Many of these crafts having been passed down in single families for generations.

> *In my own hands I hold a bowl of tea; I see all of nature represented in its green color. Closing my eyes I find green mountains and pure water in my heart. Silently, sitting alone, drinking tea, I feel these become part of me. Sharing this bowl of tea with others, they, too become one with it and nature. That we can find lasting tranquility in our own selves in company with each other is the paradox that is Chado, the Way of Tea."*
>
> Soshitsu Sen Grand Tea Master

I have found no references acknowledging that Thoreau was aware of the Japanese tea ceremony. With his interest in Eastern customs and rituals, I believe he would have enjoyed the aesthetics of tea, even though he abstained from any stimulants, including coffee, tea and alcohol.

*Chapter Eleven*

# *Early Concerns, Present Danger*

On our first date more than twenty-six years ago, my wife Dee and I filled our conversation with talk of future plans. Mine included building an off-grid home one day. We were both committed to doing whatever we could as our contribution to helping the environment. Back then, global warming was already a growing concern. We were acutely aware of the changes needed to counteract the catastrophic results of ignoring the increasing carbon issue.

In Thoreau's time, with the Industrial Revolution in its infancy, there was no idea or concern that human beings could alter the world environment enough to change weather patterns. I believe that Thoreau himself would have been one of the first to jump on the environmental bandwagon if he had the chance. With his love affair with nature and deep connection with all the animals in his surroundings, along with his distrust of the decisions made by his government, he would have loudly spoken out in protest.

Today the climate change experts vary in their predictions of a runaway earth-changing event. The real concerns about the greenhouse effect, a result of burning fossil fuels, have been ignored and denied for years by the political conservatives. In 2013, we had already surpassed the first tipping point of 350 parts of carbon per million (ppm) in the atmosphere, which if held at that number we would not be experiencing these changes. We are now at 400 ppm. Carbon takes hundreds of years to dissipate so what is in the atmosphere now will remain for generations. Even if we could remain at 400 ppm we will continue to experience severe weather patterns, and current predictions suggest that it will get much worse. The only way to slow down this carbon increase is to shift from burning fossil fuels to green technologies. We will have to begin to wean ourselves off fossil fuels immediately, as it would be impossible to make the necessary conversions overnight, or even in the near or foreseeable future. If however, we want a habitable planet for our children's future, it will require us to begin now to make the necessary changes.

A worst case scenario could be the reaching of a 3.5 degree Fahrenheit increase in the world temperature which will produce a change from which there will be no return. We are currently at a 1.8 degree Fahrenheit increase from where it had been for hundreds of years. With glaciers melting at an ever increasing rate, the ice sheets that normally reflect the sun's rays will expose darker layers of earth that will absorb even more heat. At a time when we desperately need to reduce carbon produced by burning fossil fuels, the oil companies are buying up drilling rights off the coast of Greenland where the retreating ice shelf is exposing newly accessible coastline.

*Always you must contend with the stupidity of man. –Thoreau*

As the permafrost continues to melt, it will release methane which is one hundred times more destructive than carbon in creating the greenhouse effect. As the temperature of the ocean rises, methane, normally trapped in permafrost at the ocean floor, will continue to be released at an ever increasing rate, and the cycle will speed up. This is the runaway effect that climate scientists are now warning us

about. On Independence Day, 2014 came reports of massive methane plumes rising from the depths of the Arctic Ocean.

There exists a range of predictions of timelines as to when the worst will come; experts predict a range from fifteen to one hundred years from now. One recent report even states that a mass extinction could be under way in the next few decades, putting us at the end of the world as we know it within the near future. Most climate change experts and climatologists agree that unless there are drastic changes in carbon output soon, there will be more serious weather events, including more devastating storms, floods and drought, forest fires, and rising oceans that will increasingly make more low lying areas uninhabitable.

Besides using solar energy to reduce our carbon footprint, my family and I open our solar home to a national annual tour featuring homes using alternative energy so we can help teach others that it is indeed possible to "go solar." If they are interested we talk up solar energy to our bed and breakfast guests. It will take everyone to adopt a lifestyle of conservation of energy use in combination with incorporating more solar, wind and geothermal heating and cooling methods. We need to push politicians to make changes such as a carbon tax that will act as an incentive for industries and others to cut their carbon output; also, to cut oil and gas subsidies, transferring the money to green industries. If the least of these predictions happens, many scientists believe the climate change deniers will have blood on their hands. It's difficult to be optimistic as long as the multinational oil companies exercise so much political influence.

If the temperature does increase by three-and-a-half degrees, scientists tell us we will face a mass extinction. Human beings have survived other past extinctions, as recently as 70,000 years ago, when the total population was around 1,000,000. The event reduced the population to approximately 5000 people worldwide. Scientists also believe that this so called "bottleneck" was caused by a global winter brought on by ash and dust from Toba, the super massive ancient volcano in Indonesia that obliterated the sun for years. This is different than the current scenario which could be even more devastating.

We must decide to be more active in reducing the use of fossil fuels and anticipate the changes that will eventually come. We will need to be proactive and adapt our farming methods to accommodate these changes, teach others, and band together if we are to survive. This all sounds dire but we need to collectively wake up and pay attention. The political conservatives and climate change deniers all have the same objective; to maximize profits for big oil, gas and coal companies who contribute greatly to their campaigns. While denying the effects of the carbon that these fuels produce, which is a uniquely human effect and not a just part of a natural cycle, they place all of humankind and all the other creatures on the planet in great peril. We are past the immediate fear of nuclear annihilation but now it will be blind greed that will bring civilization to its knees. If we cannot turn this around and doom ourselves to extinction, I can only hope the animals will somehow survive.

*Chapter Twelve*

# *Conservation*

*"In wildness is the preservation of the world."*
—Thoreau

Thoreau was the original conservationist. He loved the woods and wished to preserve them. His words fueled the environmental movement of the early 1900s and greatly influenced both John Muir, Teddy Roosevelt and others who established the movement to preserve vast tracks of land which became our National Parks.

In the 1980s, Walden Woods was itself under threat by investors who wanted to develop the area. This attracted the attention of Don Henley, drummer and singer in the band *The Eagles*. Reading *Walden* had been of great importance to him in his youth. Henley helped form a group of citizens who raised money to preserve Thoreau's Walden.

My family decided to put our own farmland into a conservation restriction which would preserve our land in perpetuity so there will never be homes built on the property. We still own the land, and any restrictions will be a part of a deed transfer if the land is ever sold. My wife and I put fifty of our original sixty-five acres into the conservation restriction first. Doing so meant that we would pass up the opportunity to sell prime Northampton land from which we could have realized hundreds of thousands of dollars in profit. Our reward instead is our knowing that the land will remain forever wild, and the nearby animals will have a refuge. Three of my sisters followed suit, also putting their land in conservation restrictions, for a total of 240 acres preserved out of our 350 acres.

*"To preserve wild animals implies generally, the creation of a forest for them to dwell in or resort to, so it is with man."*
—Thoreau

These parcels became part of a larger wildlife corridor extending south about two miles to Turkey Hill Road which parallels our street. On the opposite side of the road is town land that is part of a watershed protection area and includes land on both sides of the road east to Leeds, about three miles away. This protects two reservoirs that are water supplies which were once, but are no longer used for Northampton drinking water. One of the reservoirs was created when a dam was built in 1883, a beautiful arched, granite dam that created a water supply that served Northampton for twenty years. A much larger one was built further downstream to accommodate a growing Northampton.

In 2005 the Massachusetts Dam Safety Commission deemed the 1883 dam to be a high hazard, and said that it would have to be repaired or removed. The Board of Public Works was inclined to remove it. Dee and I were very opposed to its demise as it offers a beautiful spot that otter, blue heron, kingfishers and Merganser ducks call home. We formed a committee, calling ourselves "Friends of the Upper Roberts Meadow Dam" which included neighbors, friends, and family, with a goal of leaving the dam intact. We raised $6,000 and hired both a micro-hydro power engineer and a dam safety expert. Both of their calculations showed that there was enough flow from Roberts Meadow Brook to allow a thirteen-kilowatt micro-hydro plant. That power could be sold to the grid to pay for future maintenance which was one of their stipulations. Our engineers also provided evidence that the dam could be repaired for considerably less than the town engineer's proposal claimed. We offered to raise funds to pay for the micro-hydro project (Dee teaches fundraising), as the town demanded that we come up with the money to provide fifty years of future maintenance. Two things they required: proving that there was sufficient flow for hydropower which would pay for dam maintenance and raise money to help pay for the difference between repair and removal. We worked on both, and we were awarded a $20,000 grant from the Community Preservation Committee. We had fulfilled our part of the agreement.

The ensuing two-year battle ended with the D.P.W. refusing to save the dam. Their current plan is to remove it in 2015, destroying not only the historic dam, but the reservoir and ecosystem it creates. This was an exercise in futility that we will not soon recover from. We regretfully chalked this up in the loss column, but we did win another one in 2014. We were informed by the Conservation Commission, or rather found out after the push was underway, that "Cons Com" was intending to open the previously preserved land to hunting. This was land that a conservation group raised money for and bought the development rights for the purpose of creating a space specifically to keep wildlife safe. A few Cons Com meetings were organized to air both perspectives: that of the hunters who have been free to hunt on private and public land for years; and that of the conservation-minded people who were aghast that the Cons Com would consider allowing hunting in this preserved wildlife corridor. The decision came down on the side of the conservationists. Only one out of five possible areas would allow hunting. The Mineral Hills Conservation Area was spared. My letter to the editor in the *Daily Hampshire Gazette* in late November of 2013 best summed up my thoughts on the Mineral Hills matter, see next page:

---

*Dear Editor,*

*I was stunned that the Conservation Commission is considering opening Mineral Hills to hunting. The north end of Mineral Hills has been in my family for 6 generations. When it was passed on to me, I placed my land into a conservation restriction (CR) to preserve and add it to a growing Wildlife Corridor, the phrase used by all involved. I signed a legal agreement prohibiting hunting on my land, but unfortunately some hunters don't respect private property and violate this CR by tearing down or shooting through our No Trespassing signs and installing tree stands on my preserved land without permission. Opening Conservation land to hunters increases the chances of "mistakes."*

*30 or 40 years ago land in general was more accessible to hunters and the number of hikers was limited, but times have changed. More people want to be outdoors, and the landowners who placed land in CR's wished for a different use, they wanted land free from hunting so hikers could comfortably use the trails and enjoy nature; free from the sound of shotguns piercing their tranquility. People uncomfortable with hunting and guns need areas where they can feel safe. There are many places, public and private, that are still accessible to hunters, but the areas in question have been preserved for animals and opened for all. Hiking and hunting in the same space are incompatible. There is nothing wrong with keeping conservation land, especially WILDLIFE CORRIDORS, hunting-free. There is no discrimination: Everyone can enjoy this property, just not with a gun.*

*My family asks, and all in town should urge, the Conservation Commission not to open conservation land for hunting but to respect the wishes of those who donated money and gave up their development rights to create a wildlife corridor.*

*John Clapp*
*Florence*

---

*Chapter Thirteen*

# *Encounters in the Wild*

Growing up on this property, originally 700 acres in all, I have walked most of it in my sixty-five years. As a kid I would build forts in the woods where I might escape from the farm life that I would grow to disdain. Early morning milking and a stern father soured me from the farmer's vocation, so off to the woods I would go to explore.

Memories of the animals and birds I would encounter did far more for my education than textbooks in school. These encounters stay fresh in my mind's eye, and ear. In my twenties I went out on a hike along Mosquito Hollow Road, the path to our back meadow which lived up to its name given the many swamps along the way. I arrived at the beaver pond where I would look out over the beavers' domain hoping to catch a glimpse of these magnificent dam engineers. In the peaceful serenity at the pond, listening to the birds I heard a call from what sounded like a large bird. I had never heard this call before and have not heard it again. I could not see it nor identify it. It had a deep throaty, watery sound and with two distinct tonal parts; the first sounded like hitting the top of a large glass soda bottle, the second part was higher and more of a "clonk." It was utterly unworldly. English translation: Oong-ka-choonk, Oong-ka-choonk, preceded by a bloop-bloop-bloop sound in an ascending tone, as if working up to a crescendo. I distinctly remembered the sound and the answer to the riddle of what it was came to me while I was in my late thirties.

There was a program on a local radio station that aired once a week in the afternoon. I looked forward to this each week because they would play bird songs and ask the listening audience to identify them. One particular day they played a recording of an American Bittern, a bird that is part of the heron family, but smaller and blockier. They are fairly rare, and are seldom seen or heard. I immediately recognized this call as the sound I heard years prior. The sound was so ingrained in my memory it was as if I had heard it the day before.

Another bird I would hear frequently was the Whip-poor-will, sometimes as close as my father's front yard. If you were close enough you could hear the distinct click between stanzas of their song. It was a sound of summer, as welcome as the peepers in the spring, and the buzz of the heavy, stiff wings of the Junebug followed by its hitting the screen door again and again in an attempt to go from darkness to the lit interior of our farm house. Unfortunately, I have not heard the Whip-poor-will's call since my youth, probably a result of habitat loss. My wife however, heard a whippoorwill within a few weeks of this writing, but by the time she came to get me, it was gone. It was nice to know that they are still out there, and one can hope that they may be making a comeback.

In place of the whippoorwill, we have massive turkey vultures which were never seen prior to the 1970s, but are now seen soaring on updrafts of wind currents, sniffing for a carcass to dine on. These excellent scavengers, circling slowly, are beautiful to see in the sky, their wing tip feathers looking like fingers that are ready to grasp a meal. Up close, however, with their red turkey-like bald heads they are somewhat repulsive in appearance. Is this a fair trade, vultures for the whippoorwill? I think not, as the melodic call is missed by those of us of country origin, but turkey vultures are now a welcome sight in the summer sky.

Another bird heard mostly at night but seldom seen is the barred owl. The English translation of their call could be, "who cooks for YOU, who cooks for YOU all?" Or, Hoo-hoo-hoo-HOO, hoo hoo hoo HOOOoogh, with a vibrato-like trailing on the last hoo. The barred owls also have a call, which I have heard only recently, sounding like maniacal laughter and is used in their courting ritual. This caterwauling has been described as "other worldly, with a combination of shrieking, cackling and hooting compared to dueling demons." Owls can bring a bit of scariness to the night, especially for our own peacocks, as the great horned owl will occasionally snatch one off our roof. Our peacocks instinctively roost high up in trees or on our roof where they can avoid predators that would attack from the ground. As we sleep we are awakened by a crash on the roof and as our hearts quicken we hear the scuffle after the attack as they scramble to get away. The following morning we do a head count and assess the damage. Perhaps one in five attempts are successful although one night we lost two peacocks in the same attack. It is the younger ones that are taken and the mother calls for it with a mournful squawk for hours. Luckily we only lose one every year or two while the female hatches out four to six chicks each summer leaving us with a surplus that we sell online on Craig's List. At present we have nine with plans to thin the flock this summer. Our optimum is one male and two females.

On a hike one day after leaving the area I had picked for the cabin, I spotted a very small speck of crimson on fresh powdered snow. On closer inspection I realized that it was from a fresh kill. The flecks of blood and a few tufts of fur, probably from a weasel, told the story of an animal's demise. No other footprints meant it was an aerial attack, and I could see the wingspan relief in the snow, much like a child's attempt at a snow angel, which could have been a result of the bird stabilizing itself during the kill. Perhaps an owl or a hawk had been here, then flew away to enjoy its meal in the safety of a tree. So subtle was the scene I would have easily missed it if I had not been focused on the ground as I walked.

There are always encounters with the small critters like "chipping squirrels," both gray and red squirrels, porcupines and the large variety of song birds, but the more memorable are the numerous black bears, always striking in appearance with their glimmering black coats in contrast against the green grass of our meadow. A few summers ago I witnessed one cub at the edge of the meadow not too far from our house. It was just sitting there on its haunches, as if waiting for a friend to come sit with him to discuss the next areas to search for fresh berries or talk about the best stream from which to imbibe a long cool drink.

A few years ago I stopped my truck to watch a yearling's playful antics where at the meadow's edge it would climb a few feet up a tree, tumble down and start up another. Then almost on cue, it jumped down and ran full tilt across the meadow, stopping short of the road. Upon seeing me, it stood up on its hind legs and with a huff dropped down hard on its front paws, repeating this three or four times, as if to say "I am big and strong and you had better back off." This is a bluffing posture that rarely results in a charge. The time to avoid a black bear is when there is a mother with a cub, and if you try to interact with them, it could turn ugly.

There are so many bears in the wooded outskirts of Northampton that the city had to pass a "no feed" ordinance as the bears become well acquainted with those who leave bird feeders out, and some individuals were foolish enough to actually put out food for the bears. After a long winter's sleep, they are ravenous and that can be dangerous. From our car we once witnessed a young bear entering the back yard of a home in a thickly settled part of Northampton. We could see the person carrying groceries into the house while a bear was heading toward the open car trunk, poised to take advantage of the moment. We did not see the outcome, but I am sure the shopper was quite surprised when she went out to get the next load of groceries.

Another close and personal encounter with bears happened a few years ago when I was returning from town on Reservoir Road, long known to locals as "Leeds Flat." I saw a bear dart into the road only thirty feet in front of me. It had a radio collar on so it was being tracked by the state Fish and Wildlife Department. I slowed to a crawl and watched it disappear into the woods and was then startled by a thump, thump, thump of something underneath my truck. I had seen something out of the corner of my eye a split second before, and assumed that I had run over a cub, so I slammed my truck into reverse and backed off slowly. Indeed, a small cub emerged from under the front of the truck. Actually I had straddled the youngster without hitting him with either front wheel. The cub had been roughed up a bit, its fur disheveled and looking a bit bewildered. He shook himself and walked to the side of the road without limping, and there was no sign of blood. I was lucky that I didn't get out of the truck to check the cub for damage, for the mother came bounding out of the woods to look for her offspring. From the opposite side of the road where the mother bear first appeared was a second cub! Reunited, they all scampered off. I was relieved that it appeared that there was no permanent damage, and driving the last mile to my house I couldn't help going over in my mind a less happy scenario. The following night almost in the same spot, I saw the mother bear with twin cubs and realized that the cub made it through the night and was probably OK. Frequent visitors to our meadow are the wild turkeys which are quite plentiful now thanks to a restocking effort begun thirty or forty years ago. We see them in flocks of six or seven and occasionally a dozen or more. As the troop marches along they stop and scratch the ground in search of a meal of grubs, insects or seeds and when one finds one, others will attempt to steal it right out of their beaks. They have similar characteristics to our peacocks; both foraging in groups, their heads bobbing forward with every step, and the male of both species fan their tail feathers as a part of their courting rituals. At times, these distant cousins meet in the field. As if part of a long overdue reunion, they seem to enjoy each other's company and after getting reacquainted they part ways, the turkeys off to the woods and peacocks back to the barnyard. Once one of our peacocks, suffering from an apparent identity crisis, wandered off with the turkeys. After a few days she seemingly came to her senses and remembered who her "people" were and reappeared.

We regularly see coyotes, bear, fox, bobcat, and the ever present red tail hawks or turkey vultures soaring over our meadow in search of a meal. My wife and our son Jarred, setting off for a bike ride down our quarter-mile dirt driveway, saw what at first they believed to be a horse. As the fog shifted, the "horse" started to move and separated into a mother moose and its calf. Luckily, Jarred had the sense to grab our dog, as she would surely have chased the moose. I unfortunately have not yet seen a moose, though I have seen the tracks on several occasions.

One day last fall I left the cabin for the quarter-mile walk back to the house. A hundred feet from the cabin, I heard a bellow which I first attributed to a neighbor's cow. It did not quite sound like a domestic bovine, and after a second bellow, I realized the sound was much too close to have come from a farm a mile-and-a-half away. After a third bellow, I realized it was a bull moose. It was the end of fall rutting season and the moose was probably making a last attempt to lure a female before winter set in. I kept walking, hoping I would not have an encounter with a 1500 pound animal. I don't know moose behavior, but I had heard that if you come across a bull with a full rack, which I presume is six to eight feet across, you should keep a few trees between yourself and the bull's unwieldy antlers.

All this consideration was for naught, for the rest of the hike home, I heard and saw nothing. I was partly relieved, and partly disappointed. I read later that more than likely it would not attempt a charge; although a bull moose in rut can be unpredictable, it would probably trot off at the first scent or sight of me.

Another animal I hope to see before I die is the mountain lion, at a safe distance and not with one of my pugs in its mouth. There have been numerous sightings within a few miles of our house, one reported by my nephew's wife who saw one (this was her second sighting in ten years) heading south across Chesterfield Road, directly toward my farm. Perhaps it knew that a smorgasbord of slow domesticated livestock was located just through the woods between the road and our house. I don't know how our llamas would fare against a mountain lion but I would put my money on the large cat. Anyway it never made an appearance.

Llamas are actually added to herds of sheep and goats as guard animals to protect the flocks from coyotes. Llamas are naturally curious and will walk toward a predator to check it out. Not wanting to tangle with a 400-pound creature, and not knowing that the worst they would get would be a neck or body slam, or being spit upon, the coyotes always back off.

All the top predators in this vicinity avoid human contact as if we had the mange. I walk the woods mostly without fear; although on a jaunt at night with the full moon to light my way I occasionally have a twinge of apprehension as my imagination gets the best of me.

*Chapter Fourteen*

# *Slither, Creep, and Crawl*

I would be remiss if I didn't mention my personal favorite in the animal kingdom, reptiles. I have always been fascinated by snakes, both in my dream life and in reality. In dreams, they represented the elusive and intangible. In these recurring scenarios, the meadow behind our farm would be home to a dark slithering python-sized serpent, the parting of the tall grass revealing its length. I would be seated on our tractor mowing the field next to a ditch where the snake would first appear. I felt I had to catch it as a trophy as no one would believe that this species existed. After jumping off the tractor and approaching the spot where I had last seen it, the snake would have vanished.

Recently I had a dream that brought this earlier dream full circle. Writing about this early dream series seems to have stirred up these subconscious archetypes and within a few days this elusive serpent made a return. This time in a camp setting where the large snake would travel just under the surface of the ground, its subterranean tunnels occasionally breaking through to the surface enabling me to grab its tail and pull it into the light of day exposing its crocodile like skin. I needed to document its length but before I could get a tape to measure it, a large tiger attacked it, biting off its head. It instantly grew a replacement. In its weakened state I was able to stretch it out and measure it. The tape read fifteen-and-a-half feet. As it regained its strength, it slithered off and entered a large wooden box, pushing up the lid. It disappeared under the surface of the water which the box contained. The snake appeared to have given birth to hundreds of young which resembled large tadpoles and they were everywhere. In the dream, none of these snakes seemed threatening. After all these years I finely I got my trophy.

Another dream I had in my mid-thirties involved a primitive ritual where three other men and I entered a dilapidated shed with a corrugated metal roof and walls. It had a dirt floor and no windows. The setting had a Third World feeling, perhaps Central America, and the other men were native to that area. We all had a burlap sack each containing a heavy snake. We spread out twenty feet apart according to the four points of the compass. Without speaking we simultaneously dumped the serpents on the ground, as if we had all performed this ritual before. Each snake began to crawl toward the opposite person, all four crossing at the center. Our common goal was to catch the snake headed toward us and place it in our bag. We all knew that one of the four was poisonous, just not which one. In the dim light of the shed I soon realized that the one headed toward me was the pit viper. I knew that if I grabbed it just behind the head I could avoid being

---

*A narrow fellow in the grass*
*Occasionally rides;*
*You may have met him,-did you not,*
*His notice sudden is.*

*The grass divides as with a comb,*
*A spotted shaft is seen;*
*And then it closes at your feet*
*And opens further on.*

*He likes a boggy acre,*
*A floor too cool for corn.*
*Yet when as child, and barefoot,*
*I more than once, at morn,*

*Here passed, I thought, a whip-lash*
*Unbraiding in the sun, -*
*When stooping to secure it,*
*It wrinkled and was gone.*

*Several of nature's people*
*I know, and they know me;*
*I feel for them a transport*
*Of cordiality;*

*But never met this fellow,*
*Attended or alone,*
*Without a tighter breathing,*
*And zero at the bone.*

—Emily Dickinson

---

bitten, then drop it into the bag. A slight misjudgment in my timing put my hand a little too far back, allowing enough movement of the snake's head to turn and graze my hand with a single fang just breaking the skin.

During this time period I was studying Jungian psychology and dream analysis. In 1985 I took a two-week trip to Europe. While in Switzerland I audited several classes at the Jung Institute in Zurich which deepened my interest in Jung's work. On my return to the States I sought out a Jungian analyst and spent two years working with him, bringing in a new dream each week which we would work together to interpret. I would wake up in the middle of the night after a particularly significant dream and would write it down while it was still fresh in my mind, with carbon paper to create a second copy that I would bring in to be interpreted.

This serpent dream took a bit of wrangling to interpret but as we fleshed it out it appeared to be symbolic of acquiring knowledge, similar to the myth of eating the apple in the Garden of Eden. The small amount of venom I received was not enough to be lethal but was enough to instill a potential learning experience; the poison being a metaphor for knowledge, meaning that sometimes one needs to take a risk to gain insight into one's deeper sense of self. Freud may have interpreted this differently than Jung, but sometimes a snake is just a snake.

I am even more fascinated by snakes in my waking life where I can actually catch them, even though my relationship with snakes had a rocky start. I was bitten by a garter snake when I was ten or twelve years old and though it didn't hurt much, it scared the wits out of me. It was many years before I attempted to pick one up again. After observing naturalist Laurie Sanders, along with her husband Fred Morrison, demonstrate the proper way to handle a snake, I could finally make friends with snakes again. They led a demonstration at the Westhampton Library where a dozen snakes, including garter snakes, milk snakes and a large black snake were passed around to thirty or more adults and children. Some were quite squeamish but the instructors reassured every one that besides being pooped on, (my nephew Dylan was one of the anointed ones) the snakes were harmless. By the end of the demonstration the participants found that they could handle the snakes without fear.

Behind our horse barn there are two pieces of plywood and an old metal sign that I leave on the ground to attract snakes. While they're not out hunting they tend to congregate under things that absorb heat during the day, allowing them to digest their meal of a mouse or insects or occasionally another smaller snake. At any point during the day I can lift these pieces of metal or plywood and find anywhere from one or two to fifteen or more garter snakes, some close to three feet in length. This is nightmare material for many, but always a treat for me. They would all slither into the surrounding grass to avoid what they sensed could be a threat, but I can always catch one and attempt to calm it down.

Once caught, garter snakes can be aggressive, striking at whatever they can reach. They also produce a foul smelling secretion called musk that will make you want to drop it. Picking them up by the tail area (not just the tip) and allowing them to crawl hand over hand a number of times calms them down enough so you can handle them without being bitten, and if they do, their teeth are small and will not do any damage. Once you get over the initial fear and realize that they are not slimy, just cool to the touch, you may find they are quite fascinating creatures, capable of locomotion without the means of feet and legs. They help rid the garden and the area around our house of mice and other unwanted pests. Organic pest management, if you will.

On a lucky day I might find a few milk snakes amongst a dozen or so garter snakes. This snake is my favorite with its bold, alternating reddish-brown and tan pattern that makes it quite distinctive. The markings on their head can be used for identification as they are all different and I would document them by what the shape would remind me of. If it resembled the country of India, I would call it India, if it looked like a t-bone steak its name would be T-Bone. A herpetology Rorschach test of sorts. I would sketch out on a piece of paper the pattern on its head so I could identify it the following year. A milk snake's thick body can be three to four feet in length. Some people mistake them for the poisonous copperhead and unfortunately kill them while others kill them because they hate snakes in general. They are not particularly aggressive and can easily be picked up and handled, although if mistreated they will bite and might excrete musk. I always enjoy finding the more rare species, including the smaller ring neck and red belly snakes which are secretive and seldom seen.

I once witnessed a large garter snake slip into the brook that flowed behind my house in Westhampton. The snake stealthily swam toward a juvenile trout and without breaking stride grabbed the fish and brought it to the surface holding it out of the water as if to deprive it of oxygen. The fish wriggled fiercely until the snake released its grip allowing the fish to live another day.

It appears that Thoreau was a bit of a snake charmer. There are many stories of his encounters with snakes, such as his ability to remain motionless, his patience rewarded by a visit from one that would coil about his feet. One spring he watched a "striped snake" at the shallow edge of the pond swim to the bottom and lay there for fifteen minutes and attributed its behavior thus: "perhaps because he had not yet fairly come out of the torpid state." He used this as a metaphor: "that men remain in their low and primitive condition, but if they should feel the influence of the spring of springs arousing them, they would of necessity rise to a higher and more ethereal life."

George Carr, who was a local boy living in the Concord area, recalled as an adult a story of being afraid to swim with the other boys in the pond next to Barrett's grist mill where he worked, for fear of being bitten by a water snake. He was relieved of his fear after Thoreau, who happened to be at the mill that day, assured him that the water snake would not harm him. Henry found a three-foot snake and, carefully picking it up, showed the boy "that it had no stinger on its tail" and that "its head was so formed that it could not bite; in fact this type of snake could do them no possible injury."

Of the four-legged reptiles, the snapping turtle is king. One day a few years ago as I drove along Leeds Flat near where I had encountered the bear cubs, I came across some people who had been out biking, standing around a large snapper in the middle of the road.

It was the largest of its kind I had ever seen, its shell at least twenty inches long and was probably eight or ten inches tall. It seemed to be headed toward the brook and was in no hurry. We didn't want to leave it in the middle of the road, as we were concerned that it would be run over by a car, and it wasn't moving.

How do you get a forty pound turtle, with jaws like a steel trap, to move? I had heard they could remove a finger or at a minimum they just don't let go, so whatever we did we needed to stay clear of its head. After all, we had to move it only ten feet to the edge of the road and it would be on its way. If it really wouldn't let go, why not let him latch on to a long stick and pull it off the road? Seemed like a fool proof plan. I got a six foot stick about an inch-and-a-half in diameter. I thought it should be thick enough so it wouldn't snap the end off and small enough so it could still get its jaws around it.

I approached cautiously. So far, it had appeared rather slow and sluggish; after all it was a turtle. As I offered it the stick this prehistoric looking creature with a brain the size of a pea, ignored the stick and in a flash it leapt at me like a rocket, its head and neck extended eight inches with its jaws snapping; when standing it seemed a foot taller and easily a foot closer to my leg. Fortunately I was three feet away. The sight of me jumping back a few feet and letting out a howl was amusing to the bikers and they all had a good laugh.

On to Plan B. Perhaps if it couldn't see us. I had my wife grab a jacket from the trunk with a plan to throw it over the turtle, in effect blinding it so that it wouldn't know where to strike. This plan worked, the jacket distracted it enough to allow me to grab the back of its shell enabling me to drag it to the side of the road.

The bikers peddled off, pleased with our effort, and we felt we had perhaps saved the turtle. I wanted to stay and watch it crawl into the brook, but it had a different plan. It made an about-face and slowly marched off, back in the direction from which it came. I stayed long enough to make sure it safely made it into the woods. A lesson learned: never trust a fickle turtle.

Thoreau was known to hatch snapping turtle eggs in his yard, and his friend Ellery Channing noted that these were "his pride and consolation."

*Chapter Fifteen*

# *Plants, Mosses, and Ferns*

One of the things in nature I have missed learning about was woodland flora. I did learn about trees since it was essential to know about them when harvesting our forest and bringing them to our mill for processing. However, the ubiquitous plants that cover the ground amongst the trees have eluded me. It was always daunting to consider learning such an overwhelming variety, but something I was determined to one day understand and I thought it would take an expert in botany to walk the woods with us and point out the different species.

Thoreau's frequent mention of the many plants he encountered as he hiked the woods and meadows both intrigued and inspired me to learn all I could about the plants I have walked by for years and yet have been oblivious to. I bumped into Molly, a friend, at the store one day, and knowing she was familiar with woodland plants, I asked if we could enlist her to help identify the ferns, mosses, forest plants and small trees that grow in the woods next to our house. Molly is a naturalist who had previously walked our property in search of vernal pools as part of a study she was conducting for the City of Northampton's Conservation Commission. Our kids were in school together and her son Charlie would attend our son's birthday parties and occasionally come over to play.

When Molly arrived we were excited to start the survey of plant life. With camera and notebook at the ready we started our walk in the woods. We were impressed with her broad knowledge and her ability to spot plants that until then we assumed were "weeds." Putting labels on the long ignored plant life, gave us a new perspective and appreciation of our daily walks. As we walked that day, we would point out unfamiliar plants for her to identify and what we missed she would point out, as we photographed and documented our finds. Until then a fern was a fern. We learned to distinguish a Hay-scented fern from a Christmas Tree fern and New York fern from an Interrupted fern. Weeds were transformed into Deer's Tongue and Sedge. We now know Club moss from Trailing Club moss and Winter Berry from Partridge Berry. When we pick up a leaf we can tell the difference between a Chestnut and a Beech.

We learned a large variety of plants that day and I now know the fascination Thoreau must have experienced as he roamed the forests around Concord. He kept meticulous notes and catalogued his finds by pressing them in books to preserve them. I now find delight in doing the same. We now await each new spring when we can explore the woods with new eyes, Dee and I quizzing each other on plant life that previously we could only have guessed at.

Hay-scented Fern

Trailing Club Moss

*Chapter Sixteen*

# *Sauntering*

> *"I have met with but one or two persons in the course of my life who have understood the art of walking, that is of taking walks who had a genius so to speak, for sauntering."*
>
> —Thoreau

Everybody loves to take a walk, some down the street to the store, and others to the top of Mount Everest, but Thoreau brought it into the realm of mystics and Zen masters. In order to gain insight into the natural world, which Thoreau spent most of his life attempting to attain, he would travel daily throughout the countryside. He explored every meadow, pond, brook, meandering stream, lake, woodlot and river in Concord and the surrounding area. He took daily hikes, usually lasting four to five hours in the morning, with the balance of the day spent reading and writing and at his various jobs. On and off he surveyed much of Concord's farmland, fields and home lots which also brought him in contact with his natural surroundings.

> *Thoreau was, among other things, a marvelous walker; he used walking not only as a mode of transportation but also as a mode of observation – it allowed him to see his world, not just with his eyes, but with his entire body.*
>
> —Cole Swensen

Every season he would record the daily temperature; every winter, he would record the depth of the ice on the ponds, and would note the dens of resident fox and muskrats. He was not the recluse, holed up in his cabin, as many assume, but rather he was curious about human nature as well. Every few days while he was at Walden he would hike the two miles from the pond to Concord and enjoy a home-cooked meal at his mother's house, as well as to do his laundry. While on the

*I was the only one*
*at the pond; a nervous*
*chipmunk*
*hurried in the leaves;*
*on a wooden marker*
*pointing to the stones*
*at the site of Thoreau's hut*
*a solitary blue bird*
*waited; two Canada geese,*
*necks arching, swam into the cove*
*peering like serpents.*
*I stayed for an hour.*
*When the first drops*
*began to fall, I followed*
*the path back,*
*past the empty picnic benches,*
*the slough, the signs*
*to the vacant fire lane.*
*The wet pine spills were as quiet*
*as moss, and the rain*
*rained down in praise of all the ponds.*

—Donald Junkins, from
"April," from *Walden: 100 Years After Thoreau*

streets of Concord he would not miss the opportunity to get bits of gossip "In homeopathic doses... as refreshing in its way as the rustle of the leaves and the peeping of the frogs."

In the late 1600s, coincidentally, Northampton had its own renowned saunterer by the name of Robert Lyman. He did not compose poems about nature or write books on his findings; rather he was a recluse who chose to ramble in the forests and meadows in search of new trout streams to fish or beaver ponds to trap. Back then, Lyman's only access to the remote woods of Northampton was by way of Indian trails and deer paths. He spent much of his time at the expense of his wife and ten children, discovering new hunting areas. On one outing, deep in the woods of Westhampton, then part of Northampton known as Long Division, he came across a ravine full of quartz crystals loaded with galena (lead sulfide). He relayed this valuable find to wealthy investors in Northampton and beyond and the area was bought up and mining operations began. The mine supplied much of the lead musket shot used in the Civil and Mexican wars. For his efforts,

Lyman received a cow from John Pynchon "so as to show me where your mineral matters are."

This combination of not receiving any financial compensation for his find, along with the death of his wife, put him in a mental decline which gave the town reason to remove those of his children that still lived with him. In his "state of distemperature," his hunting excursions probably brought him comfort as he spent more and more time at this passion, until one day he did not return. His frozen body was found deep in the woods, likely after having fallen in the pursuit of game. He is remembered by the areas that were named after him: Roberts Hill, Roberts Meadow, Roberts Meadow Brook, and a settlement called Roberts Meadow, a part of Northampton. Most people have never heard of this lost village of Roberts Meadow, with only a half a dozen cellar holes as a reminder, but in the 1800s it consisted of some twelve or fourteen homes, farms, a blacksmith shop, a saw mill, a large tannery, two taverns, two wool factories, and the Roberts Meadow School. There are only two structures that remain from that early time, the Todd house on Kennedy Road and the Clapp ancestral home that my family built.

Incidentally, my family members are the only remaining descendants from that time. The land on which we live was owned by two families over a span of the last three hundred years: the Edwards of Edwards Tavern fame, and the Clapps who purchased the land from Nathaniel Edwards's descendants in 1863.

For my walking pleasure, I have reestablished old logging roads that my family had used to haul logs from our forest. Some of these roads had been all but obliterated as new growth established footholds. Logging roads used more recently were more obvious and easier to reclaim as hiking paths. Some paths were newly created by cutting through stands of mountain laurel, many of which allowed connections to prior roads. All tallied, there are probably two or three miles from which I can choose when I go for a hike with my dogs. At present we have two pugs and a Great Dane-Shepherd mix that are always happy to accompany me when I go out for a hike or take a walk to my cabin to write.

*Chapter Seventeen*

# *Northampton and Concord Connections: Abolition and Utopian Communities*

Transcendentalists were active abolitionists who spoke out against slavery in lectures at the Concord Lyceum, at rallies, and in print. They supported the activities of John Brown and participated in the Underground Railroad movement, offering safe haven to runaway slaves seeking refuge in the North.

The Transcendentalists were outraged when the Kansas-Nebraska Act, passed in 1850, stated that the newly established state of Nebraska, and Kansas from which it was separated, allowed slavery by "popular sovereignty." This change essentially repealed the 1820 Missouri Compromise that limited slavery generally to the South. They were also furious about the Fugitive Slave Law which required citizens to aid in the capture of runaway slaves who were then returned to slavery. In 1854 in Boston, a fugitive slave named Anthony Burns was apprehended under the new law. After an attempt by a group of abolitionists to free Burns failed, he was returned to his "owner," further enraging the anti-slavery forces. After the Act was approved, many recaptured slaves were sent back to the South including free blacks, regardless of whether they were "owned" or free, they now had no legal recourse. Years later Burns was freed after being purchased by anti-slavery activists.

The Concord area was a hot bed for anti-slavery in Massachusetts. On the Fourth of July 1854, the Massachusetts Anti-Slavery Society organized a rally which featured many prominent speakers including William Lloyd Garrison, Henry David Thoreau and Sojourner

Truth. They chose a popular picnic area in Fitchburg, Massachusetts for the rally site because it was on the train route from Boston via Concord and East from Worcester. Harmony Grove had been used for rallies by the Society since 1846, but this one was destined to be the most memorable.

Garrison had long been recognized as a strong anti-slavery advocate and as a journalist had written for years on the evils of slave ownership. In 1831, he published the first issue of *The Liberator*, a paper dedicated to radical views against slavery. That day he spoke to a crowd of hundreds against the recently passed laws that made it easier for states to become slave holding. At the culmination of his speech, Garrison burned copies of the Fugitive Slave Law, the document that sent Burns back into slavery, and a copy of the U.S. Constitution, as he believed it failed to represent black people. As the documents burned, he loudly exclaimed, "So perish all compromises with tyranny," followed by shouts of "Amen" from the audience.

Thoreau's speech, which he pulled from his journals specifically for the rally, was actually toned down from its original form to appeal to this audience. In part of his speech he made the statement, "*laws will never make men free; it is men who have got to make the law free. They are the lover of law and order who observe the law when the government breaks it*," thus reflecting his disgust for the lack of legislation benefiting blacks. His speech was later published in the *The Liberator* as "Slavery in Massachusetts." With his book *Walden* recently out in print, his role as speaker that day potentially exposed him to an expanded readership, which might have been a secondary motivation. In 1846, Thoreau spent a night in jail after refusing to pay a poll tax. He was also vehemently opposed to the war with Mexico, for once these states were annexed they would become slave holding. This action inspired him to write the essay "Civil Disobedience."

Three years after her "Ain't I a Woman?" speech, Sojourner Truth was asked to speak at the rally in Fitchburg. She was born Isabella Baumfree around 1797 and escaped slavery in 1826. She became a leader in working for women's rights and the abolition of slavery. One hundred years before Rosa Parks, who in 1955 made her statement against segregation by refusing to give up her seat to a white passenger on the bus in Montgomery, Alabama, Truth was riding "white's only" horse-drawn streetcars in Washington D. C. Her speech that day in Fitchburg included the warning that God "would yet execute his judgments upon the white people for their oppression and cruelty."

In 1844, Truth had moved to what is now Florence, Massachusetts, a village of Northampton, joining the Northampton Association of Education and Industry, a "utopian" community led by abolitionist Samuel L. Hill and George W. Benson, whose sister was married to William Lloyd Garrison. Benson and his supporters were involved in helping reform education and labor conditions. They were active in the underground railroad and were strong abolitionists. While at the Community, Truth also met David Ruggles who had helped six hundred former slaves find freedom during his time as Secretary of the New York Committee of Vigilance. Here she first met Frederick Douglass in whom she found inspiration to carry on in the abolitionist movement. Truth's residency in Florence is commemorated today by a statue, located in a triangle of land near the site of the home she owned on Park Street.

The 1840s saw other utopian communities in Massachusetts. Brook Farm in West Roxbury was formed around Transcendentalist ideals by Unitarian minister, George Ripley. This experiment in communal living featured participants sharing equally in farm labor profits, but allowing time for leisure and intellectual pursuits. It failed after a few years because of financial difficulties.

Fruitlands, another short-lived utopian community was located in Harvard, Massachusetts and lasted but seven months. Its demise was attributed to philosophical differences between its two founding members, Bronson Alcott and Charles Lane. Both had high standards for their families and members, insisting on a vegan diet and only water to drink, as any stimulants were taboo. No clothing that originated from animals was permitted and cotton clothing was not allowed, as cotton supported the institution of slavery. Their wardrobes consisted of canvas shoes and linen clothes. Even artificial light was banned because beeswax, whale oil and beef tallow all originated from animals. The final straw for the Alcotts was the scarcity of food during their first winter and Lane's insistence on celibacy, even for married couples. Louisa May Alcott's account of her less than favorable experience is related in her book, *Transcendental Wild Oats.* When Thoreau was asked by both Ripley and Alcott to join their groups, he respectfully declined as he kept pace to a different drummer.

Silk mill and boarding house of the Northampton Association on what is now Nonotuck Street. The building later become the cotton mill of J. P. Williston's Greenville Manufacturing Company. Courtesy Historic Northampton.

*Chapter Eighteen*

# *Transcendentalism and Religion*

The transcendentalist movement suited Thoreau's need for a spiritual path without the trappings of organized religion or Calvinist doctrine. The transcendentalists believed that a spiritual path could be achieved by living close to nature and not by dogma, passed down from Puritan ancestors that could hold them back from a fuller and freer existence. I believe that transcendentalism also helped its adherents to create the memorable literature and poetry that they achieved. The god that transcendentalists accepted was simply a creator that allows one to seek spiritual fulfillment by experiencing nature in its fullest, similar to the Native Americans who considered all of nature their relative, their long past ancestor guiding them along their own spiritual journey.

Native Americans honored the animals they killed for food by thanking the animal through a sacrificial prayer so that they might gain sustenance from the animal's flesh. They would honor the animal spirit because they believed that man and animals were equals in their sharing of the planet. They also called on animal spirits for assistance as they sought direction in their vision quests. They believed in a "great creator," but it was their close connection with nature that sustained them in their spiritual path.

Had I myself lived during the time of the transcendentalists I would not have been allowed into their club, being the godless heathen that I am. I have had many spiritual experiences in my life and have not attributed them to a higher source, but rather to living close to nature and paying particular attention to the subtleties I would perceive, sometimes feeling a connectedness with all things. These experiences could be called religious and would be taken as religious if I were so inclined. Consciousness allows for intense feelings, which

I assume many believers interpret as messages from their god. If attention is paid to these experiences and are nurtured, they are quite fulfilling without a religious base. Many Eastern practices, like Zen, yoga or Tai Chi, if practiced "religiously" can bring about euphoric states that do not have to be explained as coming from "god."

I believe Thoreau attained his own form of mysticism by the focus he brought to his daily tasks at hand, whether planting rows of beans, surveying a meadow, walking in nature or building his cabin. It is obvious from his writing that he received a high degree of spiritual awareness from his deep connection with nature. A passage from *Walden*'s fifth chapter, "Solitude," best illustrates this point: "This is a delicious evening, when the whole body is one sense, and imbibes delight through every pore. I go and come with a strange liberty in Nature, a part of herself."

My former Zen teacher once told me in a *dokusan* (a private meeting): "When you are using a hammer to set a nail, just be hammering; if other thoughts come to mind, acknowledge them, then let them go, and come back to just hammering," a metaphor for life in general where focus on the task at hand is needed, letting go of life's many distractions.

Being in the moment allows one to focus without effort, thereby clearing the mind and allowing it to eliminate the extraneous. This can be quite satisfying in an otherwise chaotic environment. Many people find this not only calming but having the added benefit of lowering one's blood pressure, and can be a great alternative to medication. This wisdom of the east introduced and practiced here in the west since the 1960s, could be readily offered in school classes and during work breaks to lower stress levels. In China, many people take advantage of their lunch breaks and go to parks to perform Tai Chi, a slow, fluid series of movements that promotes calm and relaxation, as well as physical flexibility. Director David Lynch, known for his TV series *Twin Peaks*, is a longtime practitioner of Transcendental Meditation, and through his foundation offers free classes in T.M. in schools, prisons and veteran groups, populations that could benefit from T.M. training.

While reading the book, *American Transcendentalism,* by Philip F. Gura, I found some familiar names. It seems I had relatives from both sides of my family who were truly a part of the transcendentalist movement: Clapp on my paternal side and Judd on my maternal side.

My great, great uncle, Sylvester Judd III, was a Unitarian minister. His grandfather was a strict Congregationalist and Calvinist who was a close friend of Nathan Hale's brother, Enoch Hale, the first minister of Westhampton, Massachusetts, the town in which Sylvester was raised. In 1845, he wrote a book that he originally published anonymously called, *Margaret: A Tale of the Real and the Ideal, Blight and Bloom,* a novel with a transcendentalist theme. The book was very critical of Calvinism and the religious doctrine of Reverend Enoch Hale, and it promoted nature as a way to achieve spiritual fulfilment. Sylvester received national attention for his novel that not only became a best seller, but was acknowledged by several fellow Transcendentalists including Margaret Fuller who said that it was "full of genius, profound in meaning, and of admirable fidelity to nature in its details." James Russell Lowell called it "the most emphatically American book ever written," while Nathaniel Hawthorne simply referred to it as "intensely American." This book was looked upon by many stern Protestant churchgoers of Westhampton as blasphemy, and all mention of his name was dropped from town remembrances. This was a momentous thing back then, as his grandfather was a founding member of the town of Westhampton. His father was a prominent member of the town who later became part owner and editor of the *Daily Hampshire Gazette* in Northampton, (then known as the *Weekly Gazette*) who is remembered as the chronicler of the history of Northampton and Hadley. Sylvester III was definitely the black sheep of the family. Sylvester's brother, Hall Judd, became a member of the Northampton Association and was a friend of Sojourner Truth.

The individual on the Clapp side was a person I had never heard of before, Eliza Thayer Clapp. *The Clapp Memorial: Record of the Clapp Family in America* states that she was an adopted child of Isaac Clapp, a descendant of Nicholas Clap, cousin of Roger Clap, my direct ancestor. Eliza was close friends with Elizabeth Peabody and William Henry Channing. Ralph Waldo Emerson commended her poetry and published several poems in *The Dial*, a magazine promoting transcendentalist thought. She is remembered by many for her book, *Studies in Religion*. Both Sylvester Judd and Eliza Clapp were outliers in a long line of traditional Protestant families, not to be repeated until I came along.

For myself, I have never felt any sympathetic connection to the church and its teachings. At an early age and through my late teens, when I did attend church and Sunday school, I viewed all church-related functions as strictly social. Growing up a "white bread" Protestant, it was easy to disconnect myself from religion. Residual spiritual needs, however, manifested themselves in my study of eastern religions that did not require a god but allowed for acknowledgement of the teachings of Buddha, Lao Tzu and others who were merely wise and enlightened men.

When the New Age Movement arrived, stressing personal growth and awareness of the self and one's place in the world, I immersed myself in it, enrolling in every self-improvement class I could. Many in the New Age merely asked for a vague recognition of a higher power. After a few years I came to realize that although a few facilitators truly wanted to disseminate information, most of them were either egotists or self-proclaimed prophets interested in self-aggrandizement. After this realization, I dropped it all and thought of myself as an agnostic. I had become quite jaded with New Age philosophy. Although disillusioned, I recognized that it had been a helpful life experience and appropriate for that period in my life. As time passed, I eventually rejected all sense of religion and the supernatural, after which I began to consider myself an atheist. This is the only belief, or non-belief, I have felt perfectly comfortable with. I do not try to convert anyone and recognize other people's needs to believe in their own god. This lack of a faith within me is quite prominent and until recently, one that I have kept private, only sharing it with my friends Tom and Paul with whom I share these beliefs, and Ron, with whom I've shared most of my life experiences. They have been my friends for over thirty years and are the only three people, besides my wife and son and one of my sisters with whom I have uttered the word *atheist.*

I see the greatest irrationality about invoking a divine creator following a disaster of some kind, such as when a flood, volcanic eruption, mud slide or plane crash takes place, and one hundred people are involved, and ninety-nine are killed. The family members of the lone survivor claim divine intervention in the saving of their parent, sibling, spouse or child. How insulting it must be for the families of the dead to have others imply that their relatives were not picked by such a god to be saved.

Often when the families of the victims are questioned about why their loved ones were not saved, their response is usually one of the well-worn adages; "God works in mysterious ways, God had different plans for them, or they are now free and in God's hands." I am certain that the families of the victims of horrible accidents gain comfort from their beliefs, but I believe that comments such as these are merely psychological rationalizations. In my belief, either such an imagined god had no particular caring for the other ninety-nine, is not omnipotent or simply does not exist. I believe in science and empirical proof, and take nothing on blind faith. For those who need such rationalization to feel secure, I wish them well. I do not try to proselytize and hope for the same from others.

> *There is more religion in man's science than there is science in their religion.*
>
> — Thoreau

Presently, thirty percent of the population claims to be atheist, agnostic or unaffiliated with organized religion. In the scientific community the percentage of atheist is eighty percent. Perhaps rational minds don't need religion.

These two quotes best sum up my thoughts on the subject: "I believe in god, only I spell it nature." (Frank Lloyd Wright). And, "I would love to believe that when I die I will live again, that some thinking, feeling, remembering part of me will continue. And as much as I want to believe that, and despite ancient and worldwide cultural traditions that assert an afterlife, I know of nothing to suggest that this is more than wishful thinking." (Carl Sagan).

Some religions have risen to the occasion and evolved. I do not include the Quakers or Unitarians with the unenlightened since they have always worked toward peace and equality. For centuries Buddhism has been striving for peaceful remedies to conflict. The United Church of Christ since its inception in the mid-1950s has been instrumental in focusing on issues such as social justice in their teachings. Gay marriage and women's rights have been at the forefront of their activism. I am sure there are other groups that truly elevate these issues, but I speak in opposition to the institutions that not only condone but actively preach the tenants of racism, hatred, white supremacy and anti-science. To his credit, Pope Francis has indeed addressed some of these issues, acknowledging that gays should have a place in the church and need to be embraced by society, that economic inequality is morally wrong and that our planet's climate crisis needs to be addressed since it is the poor who will suffer the most.

*Chapter Nineteen*

# *Ne'er-do-well or Mystic?*

For Thoreau, his stay at his cabin represented the most productive time of his writing career. While there, he wrote his first book, *A Week on the Concord and Merrimack Rivers* and added much to his journals which he drew on for the writing *Walden*. The period was productive creatively perhaps, but not financially. His most popular book, *Walden*, met with some success, unlike *A Week on the Concord and Merrimack Rivers* which not only had a small sale but, according to his contract with the publisher, he was required to buy back any copies that did not sell; nearly seven hundred of the run of a thousand. After receiving the unsold copies he entered in his journal; "I have now a library of nearly 900 volumes, over 700 I wrote myself." He did achieve some celebrity as a lecturer, but his true fame came posthumously.

Some of his neighbors thought of Thoreau as a lay-about or ne'er-do-well, as he did not hold a traditional job and spent much of his time walking in the woods. His close friends recognized his true talent and thought of him as gifted and brilliant, while some others considered him eccentric. He and most Transcendentalists were thought of as mystics. He was generally liked by most although, when his ego was left unchecked, some found him to be condescending to those of "feeble intellect." Thoreau took issue with immigrants, specifically the Irish, an attitude that was also prevalent at the time. However, he did enjoy the company of the Irish rail workers who worked on the opposite side of Walden Pond from his cabin.

His friend Nathaniel Hawthorne wrote of him: "He is ugly as sin, long nosed, queer mouth and with uncouth and rustic, though courteous manners....But his ugliness is of an honest and agreeable fashion." Many people, including his close friend and mentor, Ralph

Waldo Emerson, viewed Thoreau as cranky, combative and argumentative. James Russell Lowell said of him that he was a "poor imitation of Emerson." Others thought of him as cantankerous and bristly. While at Harvard, his peers thought of him as impassive and aloof, always looking at the ground as he walked about campus, maybe to avoid eye contact. More recently, there is some speculation that he may have had Asperger's syndrome which would explain some of his inappropriate interpersonal behavior and awkwardness. Although, when he was in the presence of Emerson he would become quite animated. He was also very comfortable with children and enjoyed their company.

After leaving his cabin, built on land owned by Emerson, (he stayed for two years, two months and two days) the structure was salvaged and had many incarnations. Popular lore held that parts were used for a pig pen.

I hope my cabin will last somewhat longer. My career as a builder has taught me where the weak spots exist in the construction of a house when subjected to years out in the elements. I have taken all the appropriate precautions to alleviate these weaknesses. Most importantly, it is off the ground, high and dry. I will enjoy my time at the cabin for many years to come, and with proper maintenance, including a new roof after thirty or forty years and a fresh coat of preservative on the siding every ten years, I can expect it to last well into my son's old age and hopefully beyond. I am more proud of this cabin than any other structure I have built.

*Chapter Twenty*

# *Puritan Work Ethic?*

I have always appreciated Thoreau's lack of a need for a single traditional career. He seemed quite happy working at a variety of different jobs, doing whatever he needed to do to support his simple lifestyle. Although he thought of himself as a writer, his odd jobs allowed him to put money in his pocket to meet his minimal needs. He worked at his father's pencil business on and off, where he perfected the process of making pencil lead by adding clay to the graphite, creating a superior smear-free pencil. He also invented a grinding machine for manufacturing a finer grade of graphite. His exposure to graphite dust exacerbated his chronic lung disease. This helped his father produce the best quality pencil in the country at the time. They also made stove polish, marbled paper and sandpaper.

After graduating from Harvard, Thoreau got a teaching position at the Concord Center School. He left after just a few weeks objecting to the corporal punishment he was expected to administer to misbehaving children. In 1838, Thoreau started his own school, the Concord Academy, and in time the school did so well he was able to hire his brother John. The school was closed three years later when John's health started to fail. This was unfortunate, as the brothers were mostly well-respected by the children who loved their lessons on nature.

Thoreau taught himself surveying at which he excelled and he became much sought after. This profession also satisfied his need to be out in nature. Other odd jobs included working as a gardener, mason, carpenter and house painter.

He had received a questionnaire from the class secretary at Harvard asking him what his chosen profession was after graduating from college. My guess is that most of his classmates answered doctor, lawyer or clergymen. Henry's answer, as noted in Walter Harding's, *Days of Henry Thoreau* included quite a list; "I am schoolmaster – private tutor, a surveyor-a gardener, a farmer-painter, I mean a house painter, a mason, a day laborer, a pencil-maker, a glass-paper maker (sandpaper), a writer and sometimes a poetaster." A poetaster was a derogatory term applied to bad or inferior poets.

I myself have had a myriad of careers over the course of my life, although a large percentage has been dedicated to house building and carpentry. My young adulthood was spent working on my family's farm and saw mill, which gave me some good practical skills, although early on I came to the realization that it was not for me. After leaving the farm I opened a small country store in Westhampton, Massachusetts. It was located in the center of town and shared the area with five other structures, including the town hall, library, the parsonage (which is currently the new library), a private residence which originally was a store owned by my great-great-great uncle, and a church. The scene looked like a New England picture post card.

My store was a replica of my great-grandfather's store, F. H. Judd Dry Goods & Groceries, which he ran in the same spot at the turn of the nineteenth century. The year before my own opening was spent researching country stores and purchasing antique fixtures such as a brass cash register, a large hand-cranked coffee grinder and a hanging copper kerosene lamp that would give the place an authentic old country store appearance. I also incorporated the original post office "pigeonholes" that were used to sort the mail for the inhabitants of Westhampton, F. H. Judd being the postmaster. In the back of the store an ornate wood burning Glenwood parlor stove supplied the only source of heat. Two rocking chairs pulled up to a wooden barrel with a checker board on top for people who could linger long enough for a game, completed the scene. Walking in, a customer was transported back in time.

Thinking back, two memorable experiences come to mind from that period. The first was the day Gypsies came to town. They were the real thing, a traveling band of Gypsies, seven or eight women with long brightly colored dresses and vests, their long curly black hair tied up with patterned scarfs. I could not discern the language they spoke, and at first I thought they were in town as part of a local performance. They entered the store and divided into two groups one group went to the back of the store while those in the other group seemed to want to distract me up front, all asking me questions using words I did not understand. I became suspicious and walked toward the group in the back at the protest of the group in the front. It was an awkward moment. I didn't want to insult them if it was just a cultural misunderstanding; at the same time I didn't want to be ripped off. They left as quickly as they came; not purchasing anything and nothing appeared to be missing. The whole experience was quite an episode for the sleepy little town of Westhampton.

The other event happened one slow Sunday afternoon when a couple came in and, after looking around, the man asked if they could pull up the chairs and play a game at the checker board. He turned the board over, which doubled as a backgammon game, and asked if I knew how to play, which I did not, and he offered to teach me, which he did. As they played their game, we chatted and I inquired about his line of work. He told me he was the mayor of a small city not too far away. His manners and appearance did not fit into my image of any mayor and I politely told him I didn't believe him. He insisted he was, and I asked him if he had any identification that would back up his claim. He proceeded to pull out his license, Elk's membership card, and six or eight other forms of I.D., none of them with the word mayor or anything official on them. This was all played out in a light-hearted manner. With the contents of his wallet now strewn on the counter, and still claiming to be mayor, he produced a piece of paper. Smiling, he showed me his proof. I profusely apologized and told him I would vote for him during his re-election. (I was not one of his constituents). Even though I probably insulted him, he thanked me for my hospitality and after buying something for his girlfriend he told me he would return one day with a gift for me. He never did come back, but supplied me with a great story of the mayor that was.

I wrote this entry in December of 2014 and with the exception of retelling the story a few times, I had not thought of, or heard about the mayor in nearly forty years. Upon its completion I decided to do a Google search to see if he was still around. I assumed that he was up there in age, as I guessed that he had a decade or more on me, so I wasn't too surprised to find that he was dead. What did surprise me, however, was that the timing of my search and the writing of this story nearly coincided with his death. He had died just a few days prior.

This is a perfect example of synchronicity, Carl Jung's theory of an acausal connecting principle where thoughts and actions collide in a simultaneous realization of the connection between physical and mental states, or reality and concepts. It is called acausal because it is a coincidence between a thought or dream and its physical manifestation with no apparent connection. These coincidences happen to everyone all the time, most without conscious realization. But, once you become aware of them, one starts to notice them and their frequency of occurrence. Jung thought that paranormal experiences could be explained as synchronistic events.

When I first became interested in this phenomenon, I would see it everywhere. A significant one happened during my separation from my second wife. While driving to her apartment to see if there was any chance for reconciliation, I noticed that the odometer on my old Datsun pickup was about to reach 100,000 miles. As I got closer to her street the odometer started turning up all 9s. As I approached her driveway each 9 disappeared and was being replaced by a zero. The very second the truck stopped all of the zeroes lined up perfectly. Another ten yards and the last zero would have started to become a one. Besides the obvious coincidence, it was the last conversation we would have before our divorce. With the odometer starting over, a new chapter of my life began. This connection was even more striking considering the fact that I was not accustomed to looking at the odometer, as the speedometer had been broken for some time. That day I just happened to glance at it.

These coincidences happened so frequently that I don't pay as much attention to them as I once did, although as I wrote the snake dream related earlier, the sequence happened in reverse where I physically wrote out a dream that had been a recurring mystery for me, and then dreamt the resolution. This is not supernatural, it is merely a recognition of the interconnectedness of things without a cause. Jung felt that these occurrences were transformational for his patients. If they experienced synchronicities during times of crises they could prove to be sign posts or affirmations of being on the right path, a validation of their intuition. Psychotherapist Gibbs A. Williams, queried, "Are synchronicities revealed, discovered or created?" C. G. Jung once stated, "I doubt whether a rational explanation of these occurrences is ever possible." I view these experiences with awe and fascination.

Jung teamed up with Nobel Prize winning physicist Wolfgang Pauli to attempt an explanation of how synchronicity works. Quantum entanglement is a theory which describes two subatomic particles that share a property (position, spin, etc.) One particle of this pair (say, one of two electrons) has an unknown spin. Its partner particle also has an unknown spin. Yet the partner will "know" when the first particle's spin is measured and it will adjust its own spin to the opposite of the first. This interaction will happen instantaneously between the two particles even when separated by a large distance, whether a mile away, across the galaxy or even across the universe, ignoring the limitations of the speed of light which is 186,000 miles per second. As a point of reference a particle of light would circle the earth 7.75 times in one second. Einstein's Theory of Relativity states that nothing can travel faster than the speed of light. One estimate has this transmission of information at 10,000 times faster than the speed of light. Einstein, who was not a fan of this theory, called it, "spooky action at a distance."

Pauli and Jung postulated that this same mechanism may operate in synchronicity. The idea being that a particle in the physical realm affects a particle in the mental realm, (perhaps an atom in a neuron). This pushes up against psychic phenomenon about which I am an agnostic but it is an interesting premise. In time, Pauli distanced himself from this theory.

I ran the store a little over a year but then realized my real passion was limited to the research and creation of the space, while the actual running of a country grocery store turned out to be quite boring. I chalked it up as another learning experience with no regrets.

Previous short term jobs included produce truck driver, cutting and splitting fire wood, picking tobacco, shoveling coal into a hopper that fed a boiler in a commercial greenhouse in-between schlepping hundreds of geraniums from the greenhouse to the storefront, and working at an auto body shop.

While in my early thirties, at the urging of a girlfriend, I became certified as a massage therapist and worked for two years offering a one hour massage and sauna at my office in Northampton. I also taught massage in the same space. One year, I was asked by a member of the Smith College Dance Department to teach a workshop in *shiatsu*, a form of Japanese massage using finger pressure. Being an introvert, I was reluctant, but I would be paid and I thought I could tolerate six or eight students. I arrived early and there were a few people already waiting. I was surprised at how large the hall was but figured that we would all crunch into one end. I sat down and waited to see if any others would show up, thinking so far that this was a manageable-sized group. A few more showed up, then a few more, and then a lot more. My intimate group turned into forty or more and my anxiety rose proportionally. To gain control of the situation I decided to lead a meditation. I asked everyone to close their eyes, relax and count their breath. I opened my eyes momentarily and looked around, and damned if I wasn't leading the group.

After a few minutes I asked them to open their eyes and with renewed confidence I launched into my shiatsu instructions. I believed I taught a good class and they asked me to come back the following year to teach a class in *tai chi* warm up exercises. This seemed to help my phobia about large groups but I don't think I'll ever be completely comfortable speaking to a "crowd" of more than six.

I had always been shy and I envied people who were outgoing and believed my "condition" needed correcting until, in the 1980s I read Jung's description of his psychological types, where he describes introverts as people who are uncomfortable in social settings and expend energy trying to fit in, whereas extroverts gain energy and are less socially awkward than introverts and indeed love being the center of attention. This made perfect sense to me and made my shyness acceptable. I was never going to be an extrovert.

In the first year of operating my massage practice I signed up for a weekend New Age workshop. Upon my arrival at the conference center, which was referred to as "Another Place," I was told that the person who was scheduled to teach massage had to cancel and was asked if I would like to lead the class. I decided to teach a class in Swedish massage, which turned out to be quite popular and many people signed up. The class was held in a large carpeted attic where I asked everyone to choose partners. Once paired, they decided who would go first, the one receiving a massage removed their clothes. This was the '70s and it didn't take much for someone to bare all. There were an uneven number of participants so the odd one out was my guinea pig. We worked around to each part of the body then finished up on the back. Then the receiver became the giver, some putting their clothes back on and some not. After the second round with everyone relaxed, it was time to break for lunch. Most of the class followed me down to the kitchen and a few lingered to revel in their relaxed state. I was about to serve myself some food when I realized I had left some of my things in the attic. I ran back up and as I rounded the top of the stairs it appeared there were some after-class extracurricular activities well underway. There were three or four uninhibited couples scattered around the room, enjoying a little afternoon delight. Without a word, I sheepishly gathered up my stuff and went back down to have lunch.

Thoreau would have been appalled, as he was uncomfortable with the topic of sex and would only enter into that conversation "if it was on inspired ground." His close friend Ellery Channing occasionally told dirty jokes which Henry detested. The general consensus is that he was asexual and that he sublimated any such desires to his love of nature. Some speculate that he may have had homosexual tendencies that were never acted upon. It is thought that he probably died a virgin. However, he did propose marriage once (via a letter) to Ellen Seawall who had previously rejected a proposal from his brother John. Henry was also rebuffed. It seems her father, who was a Unitarian Minister, did not approve of the brothers' more liberal view on religion and their radical thoughts about transcendentalism.

After practicing massage for a few years I realized I was never going to earn enough money to make a comfortable living and I needed to consider another line of work. Then it was on to house building and furniture making. During the recession of the 1980s to help supplement my waning carpentry income, my wife and I opened a combination art supply store, frame shop and art gallery in Shelburne Falls, Massachusetts. Five years later when the economy picked up I returned to building houses, which I did until 2012. Now in my retiring career I run our bed and breakfast business, and write in between serving breakfast and preparing rooms. Most importantly I still don't know what I want to be when I grow up.

*Chapter Twenty-one*

# *Death of a Poet*

Henry's unfortunate early demise robbed us of additional poems and stories of nature. There were only two books published during his lifetime, *Walden* and *A Week on the Concord and Merrimack Rivers*, as well as a number of essays and poems. One of his essays, "Walking" was finished in the last year of his life. His family assured him that they would have it published after his passing, which they did, along with *Cape Cod* and *The Maine Woods* plus other essays. Also left were his journals, many poems, and letters to and from his family and friends, which have become a treasure trove of insights into his unusual life. Henry died in 1862 at 44 years of age.

He had contracted tuberculosis in 1835 and had recurring bouts for years. In December of 1860 he had gone to the woods to count annual rings on tree stumps and was caught in a rain storm. He came down with bronchitis and in combination with his tuberculosis he became quite ill. He went to Minnesota for a few months in 1861, hoping that the change in environment would ease his symptoms, but after returning to Concord his health continued to fail. His family invited a minister to visit him for what they thought would be comforting. Supposedly the minister (other sources say it was his Aunt Louisa) asked Henry if he had made peace with god, and Henry's response was, "I didn't know we had quarreled." It seems he was comfortable with his inevitable end and with a statement like "For joy I could embrace the Earth. I shall delight to be buried in it," it appears he had made peace with his version of God. His family and friends were amazed at his "tranquil acceptance of death." It was reported that his last words were "Now comes good sailing," along with the words "moose" and "Indian," These appear to be images from one of his trips to Maine where he hired an Indian guide who had shot a moose with a bow and arrow.

Henry was buried at Concord in the family plot on his mother's side, the Dunbar's. In 1874 he was moved to Authors Ridge in Sleepy Hollow Cemetery, later joined by his family and his transcendentalist friends and fellow authors, including Emerson, Alcott, Hawthorne and their families, along with his close friend, Ellery Channing.

Thoreau had been no stranger to death. In 1842, three years after their journey on the Concord and Merrimack Rivers, his brother John died. A few weeks prior to his death, John had sliced the tip of his finger while 'stropping' a straight razor. Rather than visit a doctor for help, in a childlike effort, he reapplied the flap back onto his finger and bandaged it up. In a few days he developed lockjaw, and after two weeks of suffering from contractions and severe pain, he died at the age of twenty-seven with Henry holding him in his arms. Henry and John were very close, and with the possible exception of Ellery Channing, John was his closest friend.

Within two weeks of the loss of his brother, Henry's dear young friend Waldo, son of Ralph Waldo Emerson, succumbed to scarlet fever. Waldo was only five years old when he died. With Henry's frequent visits to the Emerson home, he and the boy had become very close. Henry would build toys for Waldo and would delight in playing games with him.

After John's death, Henry suffered from what could be described as lockjaw sympathetic pains from which he recovered in a short time. After Waldo died, and in combination with the loss of his brother, Henry seemed to lose his will to live, and he did not leave his house for weeks, staring at the walls. Eventually, with the urging of his family, he was drawn out by the lure of woods and nature.

In 1850, on a return trip to the United States from Europe, Henry's friend, Margaret Fuller, along with her husband and their two-year-old child, drowned in a shipwreck. As their ship *Elizabeth* approached New York, a storm dashed it upon the rocks near Fire Island. Margaret, a fellow Transcendentalist and frequent guest at Emerson's house, had met Henry and liked his poetry, and as the editor of *The Dial*, she published several of his poems. Emerson asked Henry if he would go to Fire Island and retrieve any of Fuller's possessions that may have washed ashore, in particular any journals or manuscripts, but nothing was found.

I have experienced much loss throughout my life and know well the pain of having a friend, parent or a sibling die. Just four years ago after I was alerted by her friends that my younger sister Mimi, who lived next door, had not shown up for a planned lunch, I went to check on her. Driving down my driveway I felt that she was gone and I was filled with dread. I got to her house and found my sister in her bed and hoped she had just overslept, but she had died in her sleep. She went the way we would all like to go but dying suddenly at the age of 59, with no apparent cause, made her passing particularly difficult. I cannot think of any time in my life when I was more distraught. I was forced to acknowledge that death is part of life and everyone arrives their sooner or later. I have looked at death deeply and have arrived at a healthy attitude toward it. I will die knowing that I have had a full, good life with no regrets and hope to be fully present in the process.

Growing up, I used to enjoy listening to my mother's sample collection of twenty-two prominent composers from both the Classical and Romantic periods. She had gotten the collection of "33 rpm albums" in the 1950s from *Reader's Digest.* The collection included a book which had a brief biography of each of the composers. One of my favorite composers was Mozart, and in his biography there is a quote from a letter that Mozart had written to his dying father. "As death, to be exact, is the real aim and end of our lives, I have for the past year or so made myself so well acquainted with this true and best friend of mankind that his image no longer frightens, but calms and comforts me." This quote has remained meaningful to me throughout many losses in my life, and I used it in the eulogy at my mother's funeral. I have tried to adopt that same philosophy.

As I was finishing writing this chapter, the news of the death of Robin Williams was reported. His passing affected me more than any other celebrity's death has, I think because most of his roles portrayed a funny, happy and upbeat character, masking his depression. His positive persona is how most people viewed him and his death was difficult to fathom, a sentiment shared by many. His role in *Dead Poets Society* is my personal favorite and with its numerous Thoreau quotes I felt it appropriate to title this section "Death of a Poet" to honor his memory.

*Chapter Twenty-two*

# *A Thoreauvian Father's Day*

In 2014, when my son suggested that we go kayaking on Father's Day, I knew just the place I wanted to go. I have often wondered what Henry and his brother John would have seen from their boat, hand-built by Henry and John and christened the *Musketaquid*, as they paddled the Concord and Merrimack Rivers. *Musketaquid* translates into "grassy plane" and was the Algonquian name for the area now known as Concord.

On our way out of town on Father's Day, we grabbed a sandwich from Cooper's Deli and a beer for each of us for a floating lunch. We then drove the eighty miles to Concord the home of Thoreau, Emerson, Alcott and Hawthorne, as well as the site of the beginning of the American Revolution. When we arrived, we stopped in town to inquire about a place to launch. We were told to follow Lowell Road and look for a bridge with a lot of cars with empty boat racks. We were able to put in at a conservation area called Old Calf Pasture.

It was a perfect sunny day and the paddling was great as we traveled upstream past the kinds of wildlife that Henry and his brother might have seen. Sounds of the redwing blackbird filled the air, along with grackles and catbirds with their cat-like calls. Ducks swam by a lone turtle sunning itself on a partly submerged log. Much of the shoreline was wooded with low-lying aquatic brush where birdlife flitted about.

There were many other boaters on the river that day, mostly dads and sons in brightly-colored kayaks and canoes. One father lounged in the middle of his canoe, as his young sons paddled for him, like a Pharaoh being taken down the Nile. Another group of father and sons were paddling slowly, and we heard the dad announce that if they didn't pick up the pace, the beatings would begin, hopefully in jest. These colorful boats would not have been seen in Henry's time. Whereas we saw perhaps forty or fifty other paddlers that day, Henry and John would surely have had the river to themselves.

On our own trip farther upstream, the wooded shore became increasingly sparse and the shoreline opened up to reveal expansive house lots where Canada geese waddled up on the manicured lawns of the "1%" to relieve themselves. We passed home after large home the majority of which had to be worth in excess of two million dollars. Thoreau, with his disdain for extravagance, would have turned around in a hasty retreat.

> *"Most of the luxuries and many of the so called comforts of life are not only not indispensable but positive hindrances to the elevation of mankind."*
>
> —Thoreau.

There were many arched granite bridges that we passed under that were built in the late 1800s. From our perspective on the river, these bridges were a work of art, never seen by the busy commuters passing above. After paddling for a time, we picked a beautiful triple-arched bridge as our destination. We paddled under, turned around, then headed downstream.

There were many Father's Day well-wishes exchanged as we passed other boaters that day. Everyone was in a celebratory mood and all were respectful of the port and starboard of their fellow boaters, with one exception. There was a father and son team that were not in a colorful boat that needed paddles to propel themselves, and their chosen crafts were out of place on the small river, in stark contrast to the kayaks and canoes. They thought it appropriate to fire up their jet skis for a quick trip upriver. Even though they did not "open them up," the wake they produced would upset a low-draft kayak, to say nothing of the acrid smell of the exhaust and the sound of their motors. I had presumed that motor craft were not permitted on such a small waterway, but I found out later that they were indeed allowed to navigate the Concord River. In addition, there were a few boats with small electric motors that ran silent and were slow moving and did not intrude upon the other boats. I was determined to not let the jet skis dampen our day. As we continued to paddle downstream, we decided to go past our launch site and navigate our way to the North Bridge, historic site of "the shot heard round the world." On our return to the launch site, we loaded up the kayaks and headed for Walden Pond.

We had planned a trip to Walden Pond to visit Thoreau's cabin site and to place a stone on the cairn that had been established for those making a pilgrimage to honor Thoreau. This pile of remembrance stones has been growing in size ever since Bronson Alcott, father of Louisa May Alcott, placed the first one. He was a close friend of Thoreau's and a fellow Transcendentalist who had helped with the construction of the original cabin. He placed his stone in 1872, ten years after Henry's death and twenty-five years after Thoreau ended his two-year stay and became "a sojourner in civilized life again." Alcott placed the stone as a means to mark the site of the cabin. The site had been obliterated after years of erosion, and though he tried, Alcott's memory after so many years was close but he did not get it quite right. In 1945, archaeologist Roland Robins, found the original site.

When we arrived at Walden Pond at 4 p.m. that day, there were signs stating that the park would be closed until 5:30. The parking lot was filled to capacity with the cars of the swimmers. Looking ahead to a two-hour trip home, I didn't want to wait, but we were on a mission to place our own stone on the pile. There were rangers at every entrance and they were very serious about keeping people out until the parking area was reopened. The lot was mostly packed by beachgoers, but it was the same parking for both swimmers and cabin visitors. We talked our way into the gift shop and the ranger pulled the barricade aside, warning us that we had twenty minutes.

While in the bookstore I asked the clerk, a kindly older gentleman, if there were any other parking areas so we could visit the place where Thoreau had lived. He informed me there were not, but said if we could be back before 6:30, when he was scheduled to finish up his store shift, we could park behind his car. I thanked him profusely and headed back to tell the ranger that "John" at the store would allow me a spot behind him. The ranger seemed a bit put out by it all, but he said he would call someone else higher up the command chain to see if he could get our visit approved. I explained to him that we had come from western Massachusetts and coupled with the fact that we were not beachgoers and just wanted to see the site, he seemed willing to oblige our request. He still needed to know the name of the store attendant and the type of car that we would be blocking in. He radioed the other rangers to let them know that we were cleared to walk to the cabin site. I thought it would be easier to get into Cape Canaveral, although they were all helpful in a militaristic kind of way. The first ranger, jokingly I think, said not to tell anyone that *he* gave us permission and that he had not seen us. Jarred, who has developed quite an aversion to NSA and government surveillance, rolled his eyes but held his tongue. After this ordeal, we had been given the permission to "advance to our target." We thanked each ranger and started our walk to the site. After fifty yards up the path, we managed to shake off the experience and enjoy the woods, although I half expected to be assaulted by a SWAT team if we veered from our destination. What would Henry think?

After a twenty-minute walk, we arrived at the cairn close to Walden Pond itself. We had brought a stone from home which originally had come from Swans Island, Maine. It was a handsome choice with its smooth oblong shape. This piece of pink granite had been battered smooth by the storm waves of the Atlantic, rolling up and down a beach filled with nothing but similar stones for millions of years. The granite stone was appropriate to us, as Thoreau had spent much time hiking the hills of Maine and wrote about his experience in his book, *The Maine Woods.*

Many of the stones that had been placed on the cairn had inscriptions written on them. Some had only dates, some with lover's names, and others were marked by initials only. On ours, I wrote an inscription in permanent marker: "John and Jarred, 2014, Father's Day." Jarred placed it prominently on the top in the center of the pile. After a quick inspection of the original site and our mission complete, we walked back to the car, thanking all the rangers one last time and wishing them a good evening. We returned with plenty of time to spare and thanked the store attendant for trusting us and allowing us to block him in for the hour.

On our trip home I told Jarred that he had gone above and beyond the call of his Father's Day duty, to which he replied, "Are you kidding, it was a blast." Sharing my interest in all things Thoreau, and just being with my son, made this a most memorable day for Dad.

# *About the Author*

John Clapp lives in Western MA with his wife and son on land that has been passed down in his family for five generations. He has been a carpenter for most of his life and now runs a solar-powered bed and breakfast and writes about local history and is working on a screenplay about the 1704 raid on Deerfield.

His free time is spent hiking the woods near his house with his three dogs in tow, never passing up a chance to sit at his cabin and enjoy the view.

*Photo by Dee Boyle-Clapp taken at the original site of Thoreau's cabin.*

# *Bibliography*

Blaisdall, Bob, *Thoreau, A Book of Quotations*, Dover Press, Mineola, New York, 2000

Clap, Roger, *Memoirs of Capt. Roger Clap*, 1630, Printed and Published by David Clapp, Jr., Boston, 1844

Clark, Christopher, *The Communitarian Moment*, University of Massachusetts Press, Amherst, Massachusetts, 2003

Dickinson, Emily, *Selected Poems*, Dover Publications Inc., New York, 1900

Francis, Richard, *Fruitlands: The Alcott Family and their Search for Utopia*, Yale University Press, New Haven, 2010

Freeman, Stan, *The Natural History of Western Massachusetts*, Hampshire House Publishing Company, 2007

Gura, Philip F., *American Transcendentalism*, Hill and Wang, New York, New York, 2008

Haefeli, Evan; Sweeney, Kevin, *Captors and Captives The 1704 French and Indian Raid on Deerfield*, University of Massachusetts Press, Amherst, Massachusetts, 2003

Green, Brian, *The Fabric of the Cosmos: Space, Time and the Texture of Reality*, Random House Audio, New York, New York, 2004

Hathaway, Richard D., *Sylvester Judd's New England*, The Pennsylvania State University Press, University Park and London, 1981

Johnson, Clifton, *Historic Hampshire in the Connecticut Valley*, Milton Bradley Company, Springfield, Massachusetts, 1932

Jung, Carl Gustav, *Memories, Dreams, Reflections*, Pantheon Books (Random House) 1973 Copyright 1961

Junkins, Donald, *Walden: One Hundred Years after Thoreau*, Yorick Books, Boston, Massachusetts, 1969

Kroodsma, Donald, *The Backyard Birdsong Guide, A Guide to Listening*, Chronicle Books, San Francisco, 2008

LaFrance, Jacqui Hickey, Bridgeman, James E., Mulvehil, Sarah K., *Local Colors: Stories of Westhampton's First 225 years*, Gazette Printing Company, 2003

Lockwood, Allison, *Finding Paradise, Northampton Massachusetts 1654-1861*, Daily Hampshire Gazette, Northampton, Massachusetts, 2004

Moore, Alex, W. Jr., *Biographical Notes*, Anaxagoras Publications, Concord, Massachusetts, 1989

O'Neil, Meghan, "Henry Thoreau and Asperger's Syndrome," (research paper)

Petrulionis, Sandra, *Thoreau in His Own Time*, The University of Iowa Press, 2012

Reid, William J., *Castle Island and Fort Independence*, Boston, Trustees of the Public Library of Boston, Boston, Massachusetts, 1995

Robbins, Roland, *Discovery at Walden*, The Thoreau Society, Lincoln, Massachusetts, 1999, reprint, Copyright, 1947

Sims, Michael, *The Adventures of Henry Thoreau; A Young Man's Unlikely Path to Walden Pond*, Bloomsbury, NY, 2014

Smith, Harmon, *My Friend, My Friend, The Story of Thoreau's Relationship with Emerson*, University of Massachusetts Press, Amherst, 1999

*The American Transcendentalists*, DVD, Concord, Massachusetts, Films for the Humanities and Sciences, A Films Media Group, Princeton, NJ., 2007

Thoreau, Henry David, A *Week on the Concord and Merrimack Rivers*, 1849

Thoreau, Henry David, *Civil Disobedience*, originally published in 1866

Thoreau, Henry David, *Maine Woods*, originally published in 1864

Thoreau, Henry David, *Walden*, originally published in 1854

Thoreau, Henry David, *Walking*, originally published in 1862

Trumbull, James Russell, *History of Northampton Massachusetts from Its Settlement in 1654*, Forgotten Books, Lexington, KY, 2012 (originally published 1898)

*Walden,* DVD, Discovery Channel School, Discovery Communications, Inc., Silver Spring, MD., 2003, www.discov-eryschool.com

McKibben, Bill, www.350.org

McKibben, Bill, talk at Amherst College, Sept. 2013

McPherson, Guy, on climate change, www.guymcpherson.com/

www.Greenpeace.org, on radioactive waste

"Years of Living Dangerously," Showtime's special on climate change